The Hitch-Hiker's Guide to the Bible

Colin Sinclair

MONARCH
BOOKS

Oxford   and Grand Rapids, M   n, USA

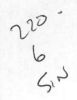

220
6
SiN

Maps courtesy of TD Associates and Lion Hudson.

First published in the UK in 2008 by Monarch Books
(a publishing imprint of Lion Hudson plc),
Wilkinson House, Jordan Hill Road, Oxford OX2 8DR.
Tel: +44 (0)1865 302750 Fax: +44 (0)1865 302757
Email: monarch@lionhudson.com
www.lionhudson.com

ISBN: 978-1-85424-854-1 (UK)
ISBN: 978-0-8254-6280-1 (USA)

Distributed by:
UK: Marston Book Services Ltd, PO Box 269, Abingdon, Oxon OX14 4YN;
USA: Kregel Publications, PO Box 2607, Grand Rapids, Michigan 49501

This book has been printed on paper and board independently certified as having come from sustainable forests.

British Library Cataloguing Data
A catalogue record for this book is available from the British Library.

Printed and bound in Malta by Gutenberg Press.

Contents

Introduction: The Challenge We Face

We don't mean to be inconsistent, yet we often are. Why do we claim that the Bible is God's word and yet read so little of it? We say it is central to our faith, but large sections of it remain unexplored and our Bible knowledge embarrassingly limited. For many Christians, sadly, the Bible is the best-selling, least-read book of all. It needn't stay that way.

This book invites you to journey from Genesis to Revelation. It won't read the Bible for you but it might encourage you to read parts you haven't read before, and see, in a new way, how the whole book holds together.

> For many Christians, sadly, the Bible is the best-selling, least-read book of all. It needn't stay that way.

Instead of looking at verses or chapters I want to map out the big picture. Nowadays, many young people buy rail tickets that allow them to travel all over Europe and spend varying lengths of time in each country. In my day we went hitch-hiking. Stick out your thumb and off you went. You did not know who would give you a lift, how far you would be going or how long you would take to get there. This journey will take a lifetime, as you thumb through Scripture.

I want to help you see the connections, how themes develop, and how one part helps you understand another. This book gives an overview: the unfolding story, the drama of God.

To start with you will need a helpful version of the Bible. Some versions are more literal, translating the Hebrew, Aramaic and Greek words into English, and these are good for detailed study. Others convey the thrust (dynamic equivalence) of the writer. These give the feel and flow of a book. The translation, size of print and layout are all matters of personal choice. If it is going to be your companion for the journey, choose the version that works for you. Don't worry about writing in it, or wearing it out. You can always buy another!

The thin paper, small print and double columns of many Bibles conceal the fact that this is a big book, an extraordinary one. In this book of two volumes are sixty-six books, 1,187 chapters, 31,175 verses and apparently 810,697 words. There were no chapter divisions until the twelfth century and no verse designations until 1551.

Here is a book written over 1,400 years, sixty generations, by at least forty authors from a wide variety of backgrounds. Kings and peasants, philosophers and soldiers, legislators and fishermen, poets and statesmen, shepherds and court officials, princes, priests and prophets all contributed to it. Parts were written in Asia, Africa and Europe. It was written from Rome in the West to Persia in the East, some sections in the wilderness, others in prisons, homes and palaces. There were reflections from a hillside and dictation in a crowded city. Some authors reflected on life in times of peace, others penned them through war. All moods and conditions are found here – joy and sorrow, certainty and doubt, fear and love, hope and despair. Different personalities and writing styles emerge. The variety of literature needs to be taken seriously. Some writings were shaped by an editor's pen; others were drawn from a variety of sources. We must take the form of the finished work seriously as history, law, prophecy, poetry, teaching, parable, allegory, biography and letter. Here are lists and title deeds (not the most exciting!), riveting narrative, stories full of profound insight, memoirs and apocalyptic writing.

Yet, despite the variety of material and presentation, Christians believe there is a profound unity to this diversity. For the Bible has a double authorship. It was written by people in their own way, in their own style, influenced by their own personality and temperament. But, in a mystery beyond our understanding, these writers were moved (blown along) by the Holy Spirit so that what they wrote was the word of God (2 Peter 1:21). Each part of the Bible, properly understood, is God-breathed, able to teach us what is right, show us what is wrong, help us to grow as Christians and draw us closer to God who speaks through what he has spoken (2 Timothy 3:16, 17). Each writer spoke freely out of their circumstances, yet, one unfolding message emerges.

Open your Bible at the contents page. For some reason, no one ever looks at the contents page. When a passage is announced, church members flick hopefully, trusting they will land at the right place. This can be hard when the reading comes from Ruth, Obadiah or Philemon!

> ❯ Despite the variety of material and presentation, Christians believe there is a profound unity to this diversity.

There are sixty-six books in the Bible, divided into two volumes, the Old Testament and the New Testament. An easy way of remembering the number of books in each Testament is that 'Old' has three letters, 'Testament' has nine, and the Old Testament has thirty-nine books, making up about three-quarters of our Bible. Similarly, 'New' has three, 'Testament' still has nine, and the New Testament has three times nine, i.e. twenty-seven books.

However, we can go further.

Old Testament

Look at the thirty-nine Old Testament books. They are arranged in three sections. Take a handful out of the middle (five), and the other thirty-four books divide into two groups of seventeen. The first seventeen books are history, telling the story from creation until the return from exile (400 years before Christ). The middle five are called Wisdom, or Writings or poetry. The final seventeen are prophecy. The two groups of seventeen can be further divided into sections of five and twelve.

The seventeen history books divide into five and twelve. The first five, called the Pentateuch, the Law or the Torah, provide the framework for all that follow and are thus foundational. They are followed by the twelve history books telling the story from Joshua (the entrance to the land) to Esther (in exile from the land).

The seventeen books of prophecy divide into five and twelve. The first five are the major prophets and the last twelve the minor prophets. 'Major' and 'minor' have nothing to do with importance, and everything to do with length. The five major prophets are longer, whereas the twelve minor ones could fit onto one roll of manuscript.

OLD TESTAMENT 39				
History 17		**Writings** 5	**Prophecy** 17	
Pentateuch 5	**History** 12	**Poetry / Wisdom** 5	**Major** 5	**Minor** 12
Genesis	Joshua	Job	Isaiah	Hosea
Exodus	Judges	Psalms	Jeremiah	Joel
Leviticus	Ruth	Proverbs	Lamentations	Amos
Numbers	1 Samuel	Ecclesiastes	Ezekiel	Obadiah
Deuteronomy	2 Samuel	Song of Songs	Daniel	Jonah
	1 Kings			Micah
	2 Kings			Nahum
	1 Chronicles			Habakkuk
	2 Chronicles			Zephaniah
	Ezra			Haggai
	Nehemiah			Zechariah
	Esther			Malachi

The Old Testament books, as well as being by and large arranged chronologically, in each section, are also arranged by topic. At times their concerns overlap. A prophet's writings can illuminate that period of history. The story of King Hezekiah can be read alongside Isaiah and Micah.

New Testament

We can apply a similar approach to the New Testament. It too can be divided into three sections.

The first five books, as history, tell us 'his story', the life and ministry of Jesus, his death and resurrection, and in the book of Acts his continuing work through his Spirit.

The other twenty-two books divide unevenly into twenty-one and one! The middle section of books, often called 'The Epistles', consists simply of letters.

The final book is parallel to the prophetic section of the Old but we

NEW TESTAMENT				
		27		
His story		**Letters**		**Apocalyptic**
5		21		1
Gospels	**Acts**	**Paul's letters**	**Other letters**	
4	1	13	8	1
Matthew	Acts	Romans	Hebrews	Revelation
Mark		1 Corinthians	James	
Luke		2 Corinthians	1 Peter	
John		Galatians	2 Peter	
		Ephesians	1 John	
		Philippians	2 John	
		Colossians	3 John	
		1 Thessalonians	Jude	
		2 Thessalonians		
		1 Timothy		
		2 Timothy		
		Titus		
		Philemon		

call it 'apocalyptic' – an unveiling, a looking behind the scenes at God's purposes.

Together, the Old and New Testaments tell one story. God reveals to us what we need to know about himself, ourselves and his plans and purposes. He does so by progressive revelation; that is, he gradually, stage by stage, fills in the details to complete the picture. Not that the later revelation contradicts or annuls what has gone before. What comes later, though, does help us to see things in a different light. We have a new perspective; ideas are deepened and developed, and details filled in.

What the Old Testament begins, the New Testament completes. Without the New Testament, the Old is a start that has no finish; without the Old Testament, the New Testament has a finish but no start.

We are ready to set off. Onto the road, thumbs out; let's start on a road that should change your life.

> Together, the Old and New Testaments tell one story. God reveals to us what we need to know about himself, ourselves and his plans and purposes.

The Pentateuch: The First Five Books

Jesus took the Old Testament seriously, and so should we. After his resurrection, Jesus explained his life, death and resurrection to his disciples by drawing from the whole Old Testament. 'Everything must be fulfilled that is written about me in the Law of Moses, the Prophets and the Psalms' (Luke 24:44). Why does he refer to the Old Testament in this way?

> Jesus took the Old Testament seriously, and so should we.

The Old Testament that Jesus used was arranged differently from ours. We follow the Greek translation of the Old Testament, written in the second century BC. Jesus used the Hebrew Old Testament.

OLD TESTAMENT (English arrangement)				
		39		
History		Writings	Prophecy	
17		5	17	
Pentateuch	History	Poetry/Wisdom	Major	Minor
5	12	5	5	12
Genesis	Joshua	Job	Isaiah	Hosea
Exodus	Judges	Psalms	Jeremiah	Joel
Leviticus	Ruth	Proverbs	Lamentations	Amos
Numbers	1 Samuel	Ecclesiastes	Ezekiel	Obadiah
Deuteronomy	2 Samuel	Song of Songs	Daniel	Jonah
	1 Kings			Micah
	2 Kings			Nahum
	1 Chronicles			Habakkuk
	2 Chronicles			Zephaniah
	Ezra			Haggai
	Nehemiah			Zechariah
	Esther			Malachi

OLD TESTAMENT (Hebrew arrangement)		
	24	
Torah/ Law (instruction)	**Prophecy**	**Writings**
5	8	11
	Former Prophets	**Former writings**
Genesis	Joshua	Psalms
Exodus	Judges	Proverbs
Leviticus	Samuel	Job
Numbers	Kings	
Deuteronomy		**Five rolls**
	Latter Prophets	Song of Songs
	Isaiah	Ruth
	Jeremiah	Lamentations
	Ezekiel	Ecclesiastes
	The Twelve	Esther
		Latter writings
		Daniel
		Ezra/Nehemiah
		Chronicles

When Jesus mentions the Law, the Prophets and the Psalms, he refers to the three main sections of the Hebrew Bible. In Luke 11:51 and Matthew 23:35 Jesus speaks of the blood of the prophets being shed from that of Abel to that of Zechariah. The shedding of Abel's blood is recorded in Genesis 4:8, the first book in the Hebrew Bible; the blood of Zechariah is recorded in 2 Chronicles 24:21, the last book in the Hebrew arrangement. It is as if Jesus were saying that the whole of the Old Testament has something to say about him. While we are looking at the Hebrew arrangement we can note various features:

1. Volumes that take up two or more books in our Old Testament are combined in the Hebrew arrangement, e.g. Samuel, Kings, Chronicles, Ezra/Nehemiah, and the Twelve, reducing the number from thirty-nine to twenty-four.
2. Some of the books that we call 'history' are called 'former prophets', for God reveals himself not only in words but also in deeds. Therefore these 'histories' are not objective (although not fanciful either),

because they teach us about God's dealings with people as well as about the events themselves.

3. The five rolls were read at five festivals in the Jewish calendar: the Song of Songs at Passover; Ruth at Pentecost – harvest time; Lamentations at the Black Fast (the anniversary of the Destruction of the Temple); Ecclesiastes at the White Fast (the Day of Atonement); and Esther at the Feast of Purim, the annual reminder of the last-mentioned story.

The Torah:
Genesis, Exodus, Leviticus, Numbers and Deuteronomy

1. Genesis –
the book of beginnings – faith

Chapters 1–11 Primeval history

1. Creation (1–2)
2. Condemnation
    a) of individuals – Adam and Eve (3)
    b) of family – Cain and Abel (4–5)
    c) of society – Noah and the flood (6–9)
    d) of the nations – Tower of Babel (10–11)

Chapters 12–50 Patriarchal history

3. Call of God
    a) Abraham – the person God called (12–25)
        – obedient faith – courageous
    b) Isaac – the person God led (21–36)
        – passive faith – contemplative
    c) Jacob – the person God changed (25–50)
        – restless faith – crooked
    d) Joseph – the person God used (30–50)
        – triumphant faith – consecrated

It all starts with Genesis, one of the easiest books to read. In the Hebrew arrangement each book was titled by its opening word, in this case 'Beginnings', a good name for it. It tells of the beginning of everything, except God himself. Our title 'Genesis' is more obscure, referring to 'origins' or the number of generations mentioned.

Genesis has fifty chapters which divide into two parts, Genesis 1–11 and Genesis 12–50. The first half deals with primeval history, harder to date, covering large stretches of time. The second part covers four generations of one family and its key figures – Abraham, Isaac, Jacob (or Israel) and Joseph, and their families. Because these figures are often called patriarchs, this section can be called patriarchal history. We will find on our journey that these stories are very adult and profound, reflecting the same issues of personal life, ambition, marriage and family that we face today. Don't leave them in the edited versions learned at Sunday school.

Genesis is a fast-moving story, taking us from Eden to Egypt. It begins with creation and ends with a coffin. It starts with two people and ends with seventy-five. The first eleven chapters have never been short of controversy, and that continues today. The debates about science against faith, creation versus evolution, intelligent design or natural selection, Dawkins against McGrath, etc. still create more heat than light. The timescale of creation, the historicity of the fall, the existence of Eden, the length of life in those days, the extent of the flood, etc. fill many books. But let us step back from all that and see what stands out.

Any description of creation, being communicated to pre-scientific as well as to scientific generations, has to use poetic, universal language rather than prose. Genesis chapter 1 is written primarily to tell us not the 'when' or 'how' of creation but the 'who' and why'. The first chapter provides a dignified, sublime and majestic picture. There is a stately unfolding of God's creation stage by stage, from chaos to cosmos, brought about by God's powerful creative word. As the psalmist said, 'He spoke and it was done'. Cosmic and comprehensive, it climaxes with the creation of humanity, male and female. All was good, and the creation of men and women was very good.

Since there were no human beings around until 'day six', we can hardly call Genesis 1 history. There is poetry here with its parallelism and metaphor. Also the prophetic, for what happened before humankind had to be revealed to the writer in terms he could comprehend. A time-collapsed form may have been used to do this. Yet, whatever form of literature it is, it stands in stark contrast to the varying mythological accounts of creation that survive from antiquity.

> Genesis chapter 1 is written primarily to tell us not the 'when' or 'how' of creation but the 'who' and 'why'.

In a world where we can feel so insignificant, this account puts space and time into perspective. They are a mere back-cloth to the real drama, our relationship with God. Yet creation *does* matter. We mustn't lose the truth that God is creator; we are to be good stewards and guardians of his world and beyond. The focus, however, is on what happens after creation, not before.

Genesis 2 tells the same story from another angle. Here, the story of man and woman forms the centrepiece. The image of God is defined as a combination of dust and the breath of God, which would have physical, mental, social, and spiritual dimensions. Men and women are capable of communion with God, yet, being creatures, are not equal with God. From the beginning they are given tremendous freedom, but remain under probation. Adam is accountable to God but responsible for the rest of creation. And woman, Eve, was made as his perfect companion. Chapter 2 remains a key chapter on issues of equality of status, diversity of roles and the nature of marriage.

Chapter 3 is vital to our understanding of what went wrong. But it does come after chapters 1 and 2, and their teaching must never be lost. The opening chapters give human beings dignity. They are shown to have imagination, resourcefulness and self-consciousness. We see them engaged in science and meaningful satisfying work, and all that before the fall. They are given real responsibility, and express a need for meaningful relationships. As Genesis 2 concludes, we see a world in harmony, with right relationships between human beings and God, between the sexes, with the rest of the created world and with the world itself. Then things went wrong!

As Romans 5 says, 'sin entered'. In a marvellously told story we recognize ourselves and every generation in the choices made by Adam and Eve. We also blush in embarrassed recognition of their quickness to pass the blame. The buck was passed from Adam to Eve and then to the serpent, who hadn't a leg to stand on! God had spoken, they had chosen to doubt God's word, and disaster resulted. Their nakedness was exposed, their guilt self-evident, and the consequences severe. They faced death: spiritual death then (separation from the presence of God) and physical decay thereafter. Paradise was lost and the long journey in exile began. Interestingly, the imagery of Genesis 3 is recalled in Revelation 21–22. However figuratively or literally you take the details of the story, the rest of the Bible makes little sense unless you take the facts of chapter 3 seriously. Here we find curse and promise, the twisting of all that is good, estrangement and alienation. Human problems are wide-ranging, touching every dimension of life. They are theological – we are cut off from God; sociological – there is a lack of trust between people; psychological – we are divided within ourselves; and ecological – we are out of step with our environment. But within this bleak scenario an elusive Delphic-style promise is found in Genesis 3:15 which would take shape in future generations and find focus in prayer for the messiah to come – the one who would bruise the serpent's head at the cost of an attack on his heel.

As with the opening of Pandora's box, sin, once released, can never be confined. It spreads and finds new and varied ways of dragging humanity down and rubbing our faces in the dust from which we were made. From now on it will be all downhill until chapter 12. Hopes of new beginnings in Abel are crushed by Cain, the wandering nomad, forever restless, unwilling to master his anger or take proper responsibility for anyone other than himself.

The first couple, divided by greed, becomes the first family, shattered by violence as the elder son murders the younger. Then society, tainted by self, spirals downwards as evil's grip tightens. It seems that only a fresh start holds out any real hope of change. The judgement of the flood is a solemn reminder that God takes sin seriously. There comes a day when God will act. His delays are opportunities for mercy, not for cynicism. The consequences of the flood are not played up. The Bible is extremely reticent about describing or playing on feelings. The bald statement, however, that 'every living thing on the face of the earth was wiped out' says it all. It leaves a catch in the throat of those whose instinctive hope is always sentimental.

The new beginning is as flawed as the first. Hardly have the waters settled when the old story is replayed. Noah, despite building an altar and inheriting the rainbow promise, gets drunk. His dignity is defiled by Ham, who is cursed for his crassness. Shem, the first of Noah's three sons (Shem, Ham and Japheth), is the origin of the word 'Semitic'.

> Capable and organized, self-centred humanity tries to organize itself independently of God.

We often focus on the extent of their reportedly extraordinarily long lives, but what matters is, in fact, the repeated refrain 'and he died', 'and he died'. The legacy of disobedience is the reality of mortality. Today we hide from death by pouring all our energies into life, and so did the post-flood society. Capable and organized, self-centred humanity tries to organize itself independently of God. But Babel (reversed at Pentecost) becomes 'babble' and the communication breakdown leads to dispersal and division as the nations scatter over the face of the earth.

The time has come for a different strategy and the long play that leads to Bethlehem. Out of the nations, one man is chosen. From that one man

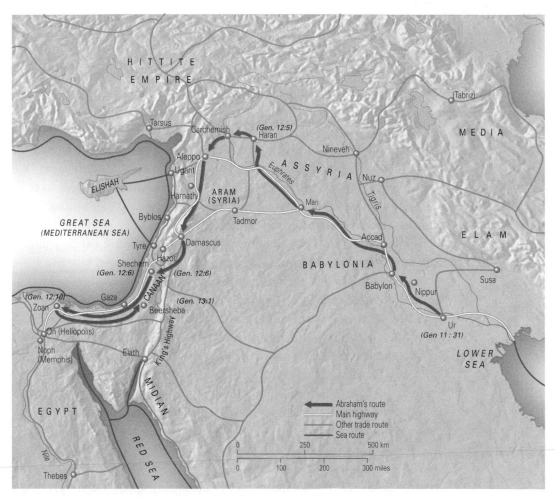

Abraham's migration: from Ur to Egypt.

will come in time a family, a tribe and a nation. Abraham was that person, the Christopher Columbus of faith, who set off not knowing where, leaving all that was familiar and comfortable, because God had called him to do so. His story, and those that follow, is not one of plaster cast saints but of real flesh-and-blood people. They made choices, good and bad, as they sought to work out what it means to live by faith. Abraham's faith was shown by obedience to God's word, as it always must be. Leaving the comfort of Ur, Abraham left the city for the country, a home for a tent, and became a pilgrim and a stranger, trusting in the promises of God. He is called Abra[ha]m the Hebrew in Genesis 14:13.

His story takes up more space than everything that has preceded it, as if to say 'Take this seriously – creation is a week's work to God and the sin of generations can be passed over in a few pages. But this, the life of a godly person, repays careful study, for we are all called to this'. Great events took place – the story of Abraham and Lot; Abraham's strange meeting with Melchizedek (see Hebrews); Sodom and Gomorrah; Abraham's prayer for the city, and the fate of Lot's wife.

Central to it all is Abraham and Sarah's faith, trusting God for a child when both were old and long past childbearing age. The story of Abraham begins not in chapter 12 with his call but at the end of chapter 11, where the litany of marriage and family is rudely interrupted. We read for the first time of anyone, 'Now Sarai was barren; she had no children'. Perhaps it was the promise of a child, as well as a land and a future, that persuaded Abram to leave and Sarai to go with him. He was given repeated promises but one season of doubt led to serious consequences. Prompted by Sarah, he was encouraged to sleep with her slave girl, Hagar. This led to the birth of Ishmael with consequences that would dog that family for generations.

Despite this, Abraham did believe, and that belief put him right with God. His story forms the centrepiece of Romans chapter 4, Galatians 3 and 4 and Hebrews 11. Finally, Isaac was born. His name means 'laughter', for Sarah had the last laugh on her barrenness. Abraham had his son and a future. He never had title deeds to the promised land, though he bought a field with a cave as a pledge of the promise and there he buried his wife, Sarah.

Two questions are raised that affect the rest of the Bible. The first is a call to faith: 'Is anything too hard for the Lord? The second is a call to trust: 'Shall not the Judge of all the earth do right?' These questions need to be answered by all who would walk by faith.

Faith can be shown in many different ways, as temperaments and circumstances vary. We are not all pioneers. Nor, thankfully, are we all called, as Abraham was, to offer back our only child in sacrifice to God. But in that act of trust, alone on a mountain, Abraham showed his belief, as Hebrews says later, that God could raise even the dead, and in it we see foreshadowed the agony of a heavenly Father who gave up *his* only Son, Jesus, to a far crueller death. No one halted proceedings on *that* day until that Son cried 'It is finished!'

Isaac was that child, and we can only speculate on the repercussions of that day on the rest of his life. He too had faith, but it was more passive. He was the connecting link between two colourful generations. A wandering nomadic shepherd who dug wells, he passed on the hope and promise for the future. The story of the search for his wife, Rebekah, is moving, though not meant to set a precedent.

The story of his twin sons, Esau and Jacob, is known well beyond the Christian community – their bitter rivalry and their parents' split loyalties caused havoc to Isaac and Rebekah's marriage and to family life. Esau, attractive and outgoing but superficial, had a mindset limited to the here and now. He sold his birthright and was cheated out of his blessing. Jacob, in the end, took what was not his but paid a heavy price for it in subsequent years. The cheater was cheated by his uncle Laban in marriage and became a bonded labourer. Yet, for all his crooked ways, he was passionate about God. The account of the ladder at Bethel and the struggle at the Jabbok remain vivid images of seeking God. These two sons represent two ways of living that remain real options today. Esau became the father of the Edomites, whilst Jacob, the person God changed, became the father of Israel (his new name).

The final thirteen chapters of Genesis deal with Jacob and his family and especially the eventful life of Joseph. In the West we are moved by God's faithfulness in preserving Joseph and fulfilling his teenage dreams as Joseph rose from pit to prime minister. A lot happened, however, on the way to the man who had the special coat. Joseph held on to his faith despite being betrayed by his brothers, lied about by Potiphar's wife and forgotten by Pharaoh's servant. Yet, as other cultures note, through all the changing fortunes of life Joseph never forgot his family! The first half of the story, chapters 37–42, tells the story the West favours and the second half, chapters 43–50, speaks to an extended family culture. How much do we need the insights of all God's people to understand the depth of God's word!

The story of Joseph explains why God's people went to Egypt. Later they would need to be rescued, to return to the land of promise. Joseph was just one of Jacob's sons and God's promise was given not to him but to his brother Judah (from whom we get the word 'Jew'). Joseph's reward was to get two portions of their future inheritance for his two sons, Ephraim and Manasseh. The twelve tribes of Israel came from Jacob's twelve sons – Reuben, Simeon, Levi, Judah, Dan, Naphtali, Gad, Asher, Issachar, Zebulun, Ephraim and Manasseh (in place of Joseph) and Benjamin. These were the children of his two wives, Leah and Rachel, and his two concubines, Zilpah and Bilhah.

Genesis comes to an end. All seems well. The family are reunited and held in high honour, with their prosperity assured. All was settled for several generations, and they grew and multiplied. Then we read that, 'a new king, to whom Joseph meant nothing, came to power in Egypt' (Exodus 1:8). Life changes dramatically, calling for a rescue mission. We call this the exodus.

2. Exodus – the emergence of a nation – deliverance

Chapters 1–2 Bondage

Chapters 3–18 Deliverance

by God through Moses
a) Plagues
b) Passover (12)
c) Crossing of Red Sea (14–15)

Chapters 19–40 Organization

a) The Covenant (19)
b) The Law (20–23)
c) The Tabernacle (24–40)

In Exodus the focus moves from a family to a nation. This is a book of two halves. Many people know this from sad experience, if they are determined to read through the Bible as they would any other book. They gallop through Genesis and launch headlong into Exodus. It appears to be more of the same and so it is, right up to the Ten Commandments. Then they grind to a halt. Within a few chapters they give up. The persistent carry on hopefully but when they discover that the next book, Leviticus, seems as wearisome as the second half of Exodus, another good intention falls by the wayside. So we will have to find some keys to unlock the second half, and, as hitch-hikers, hope for a speedy lift to take us past it all before we give up!

Just as the resurrection is the defining miracle of the New Testament, so the exodus is the defining miracle of the Old. Here God is revealed, the nation is born and their identity established. The prophets will recall these events to the people time and time again. The Old Testament describes God as the 'God who brought Israel out of Egypt'. The New Testament speaks of the 'God who brought again our Lord Jesus from the dead'.

The story itself is dramatic: rescue and liberation, delivery from slavery to freedom. 'Let my people go' is not just this story's cry but the watchword for all who would stand with the oppressed, under a host of slaveries that have oppressed people from that day to this.

> Here God is revealed, the nation is born and their identity established.

The story of Exodus has an extra meaning for Christians. On the Mount of Transfiguration, Jesus' three closest followers listened to Jesus talking with Moses and Elijah about the 'exodus' he would accomplish in Jerusalem. Jesus, too, was on a rescue mission, setting slaves free, but not slavery to the thraldom of Rome; he was instead referring to the tyranny of self, the bondage of sin and the hold of Satan.

Exodus divides into two parts, the first concerned with bondage and deliverance, the second with the organization of the rescued slaves. At the beginning we find a disorganized, beleaguered race; by the end a nation has emerged.

The story grips you from its beginning. There is great irony in how Pharaoh's attempts at selective genocide backfire in Moses' case. Far from having him killed as a baby by his soldiers, Pharaoh ends up paying for Moses' education, whilst employing Moses' own mother to nurse him! Who says that God does not have a sense of humour?

Despite his providential beginning no attempt is made to 'improve history' by giving Moses a reworked past. As Joseph is presented to us firstly as a spoilt young man who emerged to become a distinguished leader, so Moses, despite – or because of – his favoured background, is seen as impetuous and fearful in his response to slavery. Murder and flight seem to have drawn a line under his ambitions. God, though, was not finished with him.

The encounter at the burning bush remains a defining moment. Two strands emerge. First, the God who sees and feels his people's trials

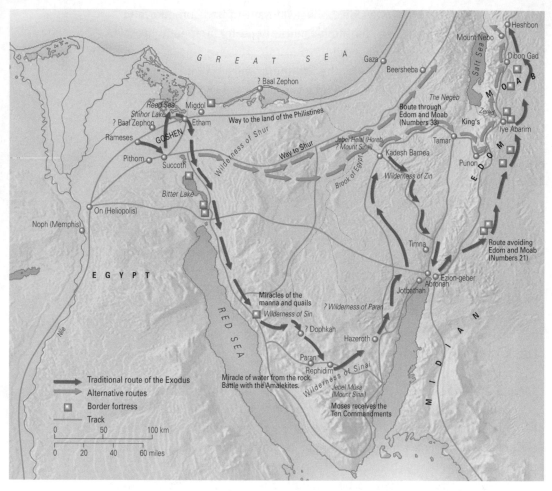

The Exodus

reveals himself as about to act. Second, Moses' attempts to avoid getting involved (your excuses have all been tried before), finishing with Moses twisting what Isaiah will later say: 'Lord, here I am, send some other person!'

Life begins at eighty, at least for Moses. The years up to this had not been wasted. Education in the skills of leadership and human management, followed by survival testing in the wilderness as a shepherd in Midian, all equipped him for his unique role. Now, supported by his brother, Aaron, he faces Pharaoh. This, however, is supremely God's story of deliverance. God is in charge, Moses and Aaron simply spokesmen. Despite the warning plagues, Pharaoh, whatever his initial reaction, hardens his heart. Eventually God confirms his choice irrevocably, and hardens Pharaoh's heart. There is something pathetic about the way the Egyptian magicians mimic Moses' plagues, none of which lessen the people's misery. Nine plagues follow, one after the other (blood, boils, gnats, flies, death of animals, boils, hail and thunder, locusts, darkness), but these warnings are not heeded.

Then the final and greatest plague comes, in the death of the first-born sons when the angel of death passes over Egypt. The symbolism of this story is not lost on Christians. These themes will recur: the need for a lamb without blemish to act as substitute for the firstborn of the Hebrews; the act of faith in smearing the door lintels with its blood at night (when blood cannot be seen); the waiting inside, huddled together as the noise of death, a chorus of wailing, fills Egyptian homes; the fear, amid the faith, that their house would be next.

All the time, like prisoners of war waiting to escape, everything is packed and ready; there is no time for delay. Then they were off laden with gold, silver and jewellery thrust into their hands by the terrified Egyptians – back payment in effect for years of unpaid slavery. These will provide resources both for trading on the journey and for fitting out the tabernacle in the wilderness.

What drama in the departure of this disorganized rabble out of Egypt towards the Red Sea! The direct route along the coast road was too well fortified to risk using that. Pharaoh once again repents of the decision to let go of his cheap labour supply, so the army sets off in pursuit.

The tale is too stirring to tell in full here. The dust clouds of the approaching horsemen, the fear of the people, their confidence ebbing, recriminations beginning. The movement of the pillar of cloud effectively blocks the view of the pursuing Egyptian army. Led by Moses' faith in the word of God, comes the remarkable parting of the waters. However it happened (and a strong wind is mentioned), the significance is not in the process but the timing – *when* it happened. The children of Israel cross on dry ground; the pursuing Egyptians meet the returning waters and are swept away. No wonder Moses' sister, Miriam, sings of deliverance in chapter 15.

Having saved his firstborn from the angel of death, God claims them for himself. But the tribe of Levi take their place and from then on are dedicated to God. They would not have their own land but would be given cities to live in.

With the fear of pursuit over, any future threat came from the surrounding tribes. Though small by comparison with the Egyptians, they were intimidating enough. A small standing army is set up and Joshua emerges as military leader. When conflict occurs, Joshua earns his spurs as they win their first skirmish against Amalek. However, alongside his fighting he learns the importance of Moses' prayers. He begins his apprenticeship to become Moses' successor.

The journey to Sinai was full of incident and took two months (about the period from Passover to Pentecost). Hence Pentecost would become not only a celebration of harvest's first fruits, but also when the people gave thanks for the Law.

On the way, Moses learned that leading God's people is never easy! They passed Marah, where the bitter waters were made sweet (chapter 15), and the Desert of Sin, where they grumbled (not for the last time). God provided manna (wafer-like bread) in the wilderness and quails to vary their diet (chapter 16). At Rephidim water was provided from a rock (chapter 17).

They come to Mount Sinai, looming stark and menacing, and camp is struck. It is time for a nation to be shaped. So the action stops for a whole year. We stay at the foot of this mountain for fifty-eight chapters (Exodus 19 – Numbers 10), having so far read only sixty-eight chapters. Much as the mountain is to be admired, everything in us feels that a bit of judicious editing is called for. We face chapter after chapter of laws, regulations, building instructions, rules of worship, feast days and the like. How do we get anything out of this?

> Three key topics of the second half of Exodus are covenant, law and tabernacle.

It helps to focus on three key topics that make up the second half of Exodus, ideas that will help us on our journey and which find fulfilment in the New Testament – covenant, law and tabernacle. All were given by God to help those who separated from Egypt become sanctified to God and create a distinct national testimony.

Covenant

'Old Testament' could equally be translated 'Old Covenant'. The Bible emphasizes the special relationship between God and his people. There were earlier covenants, however. Apart from the general promise in Eden (Genesis 3:15), the first such covenant was made with Noah after the flood. The sign and guarantee of God's commitment was the rainbow, which promised fruitfulness and protection from future catastrophe by water. Then came the covenant made with Abraham, firstly in Genesis 12 and spelt out in chapters 13, 15 and 17. Here Abraham is promised a land (Canaan, in which he lived but which he never possessed), a family (Isaac and then the children of Israel), and prosperity (which he did know in his lifetime). In return, the sign of the covenant was male circumcision. Later in 2 Samuel 7 the covenant is made with David, speaking of a temple, a throne and a kingdom. Finally, in Jeremiah 31, the prophet looks forward to a new covenant of grace and forgiveness by which people can know God directly. This hope is taken up in Hebrews 8.

The most prominent of all the covenant agreements, however, is established in Exodus. Here God chooses a nation to be a visual aid and bridge to help other nations find their way to him. As a 'kingdom of priests and a holy nation' (Exodus 19:6), they were to set a distinct pattern of how to live and whom to live for. This description is taken up by Peter (1 Peter 2:5) as the church's calling. Tragically, Israel took their calling as a sign of privilege, not of responsibility. They presumed on God's favour, took pride in it, and despised others. All too often they used their distinctiveness as a barrier, not a bridge, using it to criticize rather than to attract others. The lessons for us are obvious!

> As a 'kingdom of priests and a holy nation', they were to set a distinct pattern of how to live and whom to live for.

For Israel, the promise was that God would be their God and they his people. Clear guidance would be given on how to worship God, how to live before him, and how to work this out in their relationships. God's instruction would be comprehensive, covering their dealings with one another, and with aliens and strangers. The problem, then and now, is that there is a world of difference between knowing what to do and actually doing it.

Law

There are a great number of laws and regulations given as a whole judicial system is set up, within the bounds of which they agree to live. These move from moral imperatives to sentencing policy, from hygiene arrangements (especially for desert nomads), to building regulations (for when they settle in the land).

However, we can divide the law into three categories: ceremonial (all the laws relating to worship and sacrifice), civil (how they should operate as a nation), and moral (especially the Ten Commandments).

The ceremonial laws, although interesting (sometimes) and instructive (occasionally), are now obsolete. They have largely been fulfilled in Christ. The Temple was his body; he is our great high priest; and he paid the ultimate sacrifice, once for all, when he died as the Lamb of God to take away the sin of the world. Other ceremonial laws, especially food laws, Christ declared obsolete. In practice they made sense in a Middle Eastern climate and the prevailing hygiene conditions, lacking as it did fridges, freezers and sell-by dates.

The civil law was geared towards the nation of Israel, which, despite claims, was unlike any other nation before or since, being both a nation and a church simultaneously. Although some societies have aspired to this, there is normally a division between church and state, with the relationship varying from church to church and country to country. However, these laws are still illustrative of how principles of righteousness and justice might work out in other cultures and times. We still believe in the importance of law in governing nations, though we have learned that great care needs be taken to ensure that good laws are created and correctly enforced.

Finally, there is the moral law, challenging each person directly. This spells out the boundaries within which we should live before God and our neighbour. Here the great words of God still apply, though the tone in which they are spoken matters as much as the truth they convey. The moral law has two sections: the first five commandments define our relationship with God and how our love for him might best be expressed. The second five deal with loving our neighbour in practical areas of life, marriage, honesty, truthfulness and desire.

> The ceremonial laws, although interesting (sometimes) and instructive (occasionally), are now obsolete. They have largely been fulfilled in Christ.

Tabernacle

The Bible devotes fifty chapters to the tabernacle, its construction and functioning in Exodus and Leviticus. The tent would be carried before the people when on the move and set in the centre of the people when camped. From it could be seen, at times, a pillar of cloud by day and pillar of fire by night. It embodied the presence of God among them, his glory – his *Shekhinah*.

Later it would be the prototype for various temples built by Solomon,

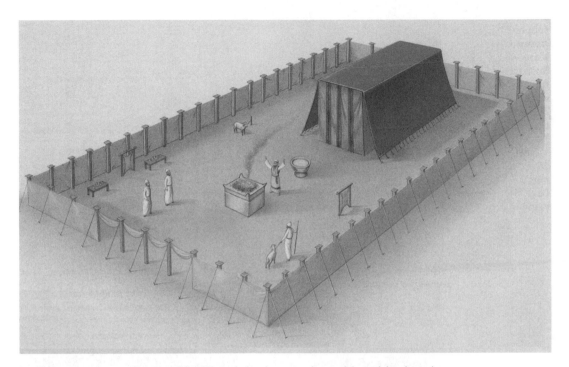

The Tabernacle

by the returning exiles and by Herod. Its beauty, its gold and its jewels made it stand out from the rest of the camp and it was designed to guide the way we should worship.

It was never to be approached casually, but with reverence. The first object you encountered was an altar, on which sacrifice was made for sin by the priest. Sacrifice was the principle of acceptance by God. Beyond that was a basin for washing, emphasizing the importance of clean hands and clean hearts.

Inside the courtyard was an inner tent divided into two rooms, the outer one being twice the size of the inner. In the outer room, the holy place, were three pieces of furniture. Firstly there was a bowl for burning incense. This was a symbol of prayer and worship, sending a fragrance to heaven that could be seen and smelt. Secondly there was a table on which bread was placed. This reminded the people that God wanted to enjoy fellowship with them, and of the importance of hospitality. Finally there was a golden lampstand, which both lit the place up as God lit up the camp and reminded Israel to be a light to the surrounding nations.

In the inner room, separated off by a veil, was the most holy place, or in Hebrew 'the holy of holies' (Hebrew has no form for a superlative). No

Plan of the
Tabernacle

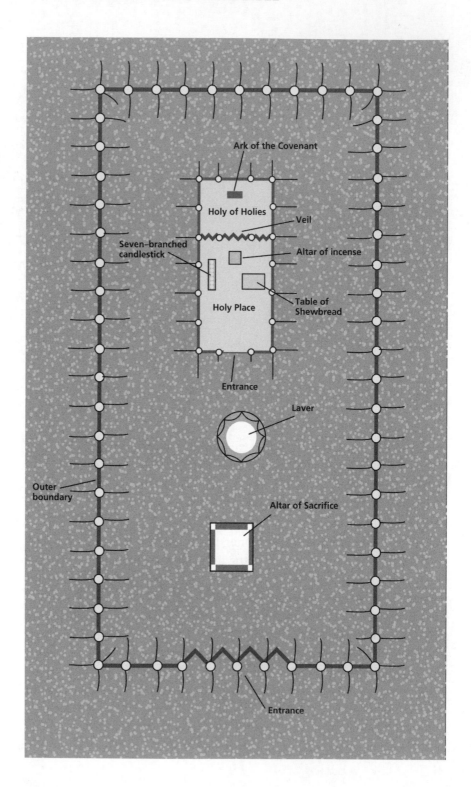

artificial light lit up this room; the only light came from the glory of God himself. Only the high priest could go into this place, and then only once a year. Inside was a wooden chest over which were carved two cherubim (angels). In this chest were placed, over time, symbols of their story: Aaron's rod, which budded when his right as high priest was challenged, a pot of manna (God's provision), and supremely the two stone tablets on which were carved the Ten Commandments.

For the Christian the veil that isolated the holy of holies from the people has been torn apart. Now anyone can come directly to God, through Christ. But we must never forget the sacrificial cost paid to open up this way to God, or the need for confession and clean hands. Prayer, fellowship and the desire for faithful witness are still the marks of the genuine worshipper today. We still make the hearing and response to God's word central to our worship, whatever our liturgical tradition.

One final story we must mention. Moses was up the mountain speaking with God. Halfway down, keeping lonely vigil, was Joshua. The others, wearied by now, were left behind to wait. Familiar with Egypt's ornate idols, they asked Aaron for some token of God's presence. Aaron, not the last political leader to sacrifice integrity for expediency, used some of the wealth taken from Egypt to make a golden calf as a focus for their worship. Like all such objects it twisted in their hands and debased and corrupted them. Israel, supposedly monotheistic, would prove to be incurably idolatrous until they were purged by the exile. Moses heard the noise from the camp as he came down the mountain, thought they were under attack, and hurried to their aid. He was horrified to see what they had done, destroyed the golden calf and pleaded with God not to judge them. God's people broke the covenant, even before it had been fully ratified. Moses' passionate prayers for his people have echoes throughout the Old and New Testament.

Let me say a word about how the last four books of the Pentateuch fit together.

Exodus, Leviticus, Numbers and Deuteronomy

If Exodus tells the story of how Israel got out of Egypt, Leviticus outlines the process of getting Egypt out of Israel. Exodus, Leviticus and Numbers provide details of the teaching at Mount Sinai, whereas

Deuteronomy, written to the next generation, summarizes it and applies it to this generation on the banks of the Jordan, in the form of Moses' final discourse.

The relationship of Exodus, Leviticus and Numbers to Deuteronomy is similar to the relationship of Matthew, Mark and Luke to John. The first three books focus on the story and the final one stands back and reflects on the deeper meaning of what has happened.

So let us move forward to one of the most neglected books in the Old Testament, Leviticus – not the catchiest title! The title refers to the key role the Levites played in ordering the worship of the people of God.

3. Leviticus – A handbook of the priests – communion

Chapters 1–10 Way to God by sacrifice – a privilege

1. The offerings (1–7)
2. The priesthood (8–10)

Chapters 11–27 Walk with God by sanctification – the practice

1. Purity (11–22)
    ceremonial (11–15)
    inward – Day of Atonement (16)
    moral (17–22) (i.e. holiness)
2. Feasts (23–24)
3. Final instructions (25–27)

For those who like action, this would not be their first choice of book. It covers only one month of Israel's history but it seems a lot longer! It is not often preached on today, so remains a closed book to most.

Its broad structure is worth noting. The book divides into two. The first part is concerned with how human beings get right with God. Two things are needed for this to happen. Firstly, a sacrifice must be made, a price paid for wrongdoing. Then a priest needs to act as mediator, representing the people to God and God to the people. Getting right with him, however, is only the beginning.

The second part focuses on our walk with God, once we are in a right relationship. It is concerned with heart as well as life, and inner purity not just outward conformity. It also aims to establish reminders (which later became known as 'means of grace') that place people's lives in the bigger framework of God's story. This is done through a pattern of feasts and festivals that would remind the community of their story and their roots (compare the Christian year).

Let me show its relevance by looking at the offerings, five of which are mentioned in chapters 1–7. Just as the tabernacle was a visual aid on how to approach God, so the offerings are a teaching aid to help us to get right and stay right with God.

Imagine that you do something wrong; you impulsively say or do something wrong. You regret it immediately, but the damage has been done and you feel ashamed. What you have done has implications both for the person involved and for your relationship with God. You can apologize to the person you insulted and make restitution, but there are deeper issues to be addressed. (It is worth saying that the sacrificial system is primarily concerned with unintentional wrongdoing, not with premeditated evil, for which there was no forgiveness under the Old Testament sacrificial system.)

> The second part of Leviticus is concerned with heart as well as life, and inner purity not just outward conformity.

You go to the priest and explain. He says you should make a guilt offering to express sorrow for doing something wrong. Your desire is for forgiveness. You pay for the appropriate sacrifice to be made on your behalf and go home reassured – right with your neighbour and right with God.

During the night you cannot sleep for, though forgiven, you remember other occasions when you have gone wrong. You are not a sinner just because you have sinned; you sin *because* you are a sinner. You return to the priest and explain that the problem is more deep-rooted than an occasional act. Reassurance is found and help offered in the form of another sacrifice with a deeper meaning. A sin offering is required, recognizing the need not just for forgiveness for what you have done but for pardon for who you are. In both these sacrifices you are looking for cleansing.

The past is fully dealt with, but can things ever be the same again? In a family, when something goes wrong it is dealt with, forgiven and forgotten, but from then on there can be a subtle change in the atmosphere. You want the relationship with God to be restored to what it was before the problem occurred. God has provided for this condition, and the priest explains that a peace or fellowship offering is needed. To the Jews, peace (*shalom*) meant not just the absence of conflict but healthy relationships. This offering went beyond cleansing to communion – being comfortable in the presence of God.

So the past has been dealt with and the present restored. You are rejoicing. Life is better than it has ever been. You ask the priest how you can show God your thankfulness for his goodness to you. This requires another sacrifice: the meal, or grain offering. It was like sharing a meal, enjoying hospitality with the divinity. Hospitality is central in biblical thought. A home is for sharing; it is not a fortress of personal space, from which we ward off cold-callers with a grunt.

> To the Jews, peace (*shalom*) meant not just the absence of conflict but healthy relationships.

All has ended well. It could end here, and for many it would. But our pilgrim is in a different league. He reflects on God's amazing grace and his wonderful provision. If God has given everything to him it would be churlish not to respond. He goes back to make a final grand gesture, an act of commitment and consecration. He watches as a burnt offering is made by the priest. All is burnt up; nothing is left. The final stage is full surrender and this he does gladly, willingly and soberly.

I think that process is full of profound psychological insight into being set free from our past, sorted in the present and focused for the future, and in itself makes Leviticus worth studying.

Annual Feasts

Leviticus describes a calendar of annual feasts that shaped the life of the nation. These were kept, to varying degrees, throughout the Old Testament, sometimes lapsing and being reintroduced in times of spiritual renewal. They could be done as a great show, in the hope of 'trading off' religious observance for moral and social disobedience. When that happened the prophets had plenty to say. But at heart they were reminders of all God had done for them.

Of all the feasts and festivals, three stood out, and all male Jews within a certain distance were expected to journey to Jerusalem to keep these feasts. But obligation is not required for a party! People came from far further abroad to share in these great defining national moments.

First was New Year festival, the Feast of Passover telling the exodus story. People would gather in households to remember their liberation and at 3 p.m. in homes, in the tabernacle and later in the Temple, the lamb was slain (compare the time Jesus died).

Fifty days later came Pentecost. Thanks were given for the Law. Law follows deliverance and finds its timing from the date of Passover. For Christians, Pentecost marks the giving of the Spirit who writes God's law on our hearts. The link to Passover (Easter) remains, for what Christ achieved *for* us on the cross, the Spirit now applies *in* us, making what happened there and then relevant for us here and now.

Finally came the Feast of Tabernacles. People left their homes for makeshift tents (easier to do in a warm, dry climate), to remind them that once they had lived in the wilderness. God had fulfilled his promise and brought them into the Promised Land. With that blessing was also the reminder – fail to live as God's people and the land, given to you in trust, will be taken from you again – as indeed it would be.

The exuberance of this final festival is not just the natural response to the fun of 'camping out'. It followed the most solemn day of the year, the Day of Atonement, the only day when the high priest went into the holy of holies to make atonement for the sins of the people. You could sense its solemnity, a day of reflection and penitence for personal, social and national sins. There was also a degree of apprehension: suppose God did not accept their atonement and punished them for their disobedience? Suppose he withdrew his presence, leaving them without identity or reason for existence? Can you understand why, if you could get through that day, the celebrations would be intense?

I hope that is enough to make you dip into Leviticus. Please don't try to find hidden meanings in every part, as some Christians have done, and so fail to hear the cries of a needy world or the call to mission and social action.

CARDIFF
CAERDYDD

4. Numbers – the wilderness wanderings – punishment and preservation

The fourth book is unimaginatively called 'Numbers'. Various lists of people are included that are a challenge to read aloud. Yet it says people matter, names count, each of us has a part in God's great purposes.

The original Hebrew title 'In the Wilderness' is far more suggestive. Numbers tells a graphic story of missed opportunity and wasted lives.

Chapters 1–10   Preparation for the journey

Chapters 11–14 Disaffection on the journey (Kadesh Barnea, 10–13)

Chapters 15–19 Interruption of the journey

Chapters 20–36   Returning to the journey

To move such a large company requires detailed logistics. Order and organization are necessary and clear communication has to be maintained so that everyone understands what is going to happen. Would that all churches understood this when going through a process of change!

There were also religious ceremonies to undertake for this consecrated people. Finally, all done, they set off on the shortest, most direct route to Canaan. Then it all began to unravel!

Twelve spies were sent into the land. Their report agreed on the facts but differed greatly in interpretation. The majority report (majorities are not always right) spoke warmly of the land in regard to its potential. However, the people in the land were strong and their cities well fortified. A group of slaves, ill-armed, ill-trained and inexperienced, could not hope to overcome them. It was giants against grasshoppers.

Recognize reality, cut your losses and temper your ambitions, they advised.

The minority report, provided by Joshua and Caleb, did not question the facts. But they took God seriously. So what if there appeared to be giants? From God's perspective, giants seem like grasshoppers. God had called them to advance and promised them the land: end of story. They had to go forward in faith believing the Lord would fight for them.

The people, though, responded with fear, not faith, and drew back. Doubting God, they sealed their fate. The people who had witnessed the plagues and the Passover, the crossing of the Red Sea and the defeat of Amalek faltered. They had seen God provide manna and water, and trembled when thunder and lightning covered Mount Sinai, but that was not enough. Do not believe that an experience of God removes all doubts. We have poor memories and too often a feeble faith.

> ... people matter, names count, each of us has a part in God's great purposes.

Forty years, in round terms, were then spent wandering round in circles moving from Mount Sinai to the Plain of Moab. Nothing of note happened, so nothing was recorded. Between chapter 19 and chapter 20 there is a gap of some thirty-eight years. How sad to live wasted lives going nowhere, going round in circles. So we are told of their first years and their fatal choices, and the final year when the next generation regrouped for a second chance; in between, there is nothing. Among the stories recorded are Korah's rebellion, the budding of Aaron's staff (chapter 17), the bronze snake (chapter 21, compare John 3:14 and 15), and the mysterious story of Balaam the prophet (chapters 22–25), all referred to in the New Testament. In this book we read of the deaths of Miriam, Moses' sister, and then of Aaron, Moses' brother, the first high priest. Overall it is a depressing book, as are the lives of the people, who, given a chance to risk their lives with God, prefer to grumble and go nowhere. Various judgements fall on the people as earthquakes (chapter 16) plagues (chapter 16), snakes (chapter 21) and epidemics (chapter 25) wreak havoc in their community. Finally, the nation, reformed as an army, gain minor victories over Canaanites, King Sihon of the Amorites, King Og of Bashan, Balaam and the Midianites, preparing them for bigger battles ahead.

5. Deuteronomy –
the word we need – obedience

Jesus quotes from Deuteronomy when tempted in the wilderness. Jesus' encounter with Satan was not a text-pelting encounter ('my verse against yours'). He carefully selected appropriate truths from Deuteronomy. For Jesus, like the people of God earlier, found himself in the desert preparing to launch out on his life's work, and needing to trust God for all that lay ahead.

Chapters 1–4 Way reviewed – a reflection on history

Chapters 5–16 Work recalled – modified and adapted for new setting

Chapters 27–30 Warnings recited and covenant reaffirmed

Chapters 31–34 Warriors rewarded – song, blessing, death

Deuteronomy means 'second law', for the law of God given at Mount Sinai is restated to the next generation. The story from Egypt to the Jordan is told in summary form. Moses wants the details to be clear, especially the lessons learned in the barren years. To paraphrase George Santayana (1863–1952), those who do not learn from history are often fated to repeat it. Some have called this book the most spiritual book in the Old Testament. It is a mixture of history, law, and prophecy. Above all it is a sermon, which shows how a deep experience of God works itself out in daily life.

The law of God, like all good law, is not static and fixed, but needs to apply to changing situations and needs. The principles behind it remain the same. After repeating (though not word for word) the Ten Commandments in chapter 5, Moses teaches the Jewish foundational truth in 6:4–8 with the *Shema*: 'Hear, O Israel: the Lord our God, the Lord is one. Love the Lord your God with all your heart and with all your soul and with all your strength.'

Detailed instructions are laid down for the next phase, and reassurances given that the battle is the Lord's. They are not being given the land because there is anything special about them, but because of the wickedness of the nations living there. When they inherit the land they must be different, (chapter 9), though their track record is not impressive!

Finally comes the time to renew the covenant, recognizing the blessings that follow obedience and the dire consequences of disobedience. The people pledge their future; the dice are cast. A new situation calls for a new leader. Moses, in a moment of temper, had forfeited his right to lead the people into the Promised Land. Yet his passing will be honoured and he will at least see the land

> Above all [Deuteronomy] is a sermon, which shows how a deep experience of God works itself out in daily life.

before he dies. The succession is secured (something we are far less good at doing in church circles), and a new leader is appointed. Joshua has served a long apprenticeship, in battle, up the mountain and around the tabernacle. He is ready for new responsibilities. From the adult generation who left Egypt only he, with Caleb, will go into the land, for they alone trusted God. One leader, Moses (statesman, seer, singer and saint), is honoured by death alone with God, the other by his appointment before the people. So the Torah concludes with the people camped on the plain of Shittim, the River Jordan and the inhabitants of Canaan ahead!

In summary the message of this book is 'Take God seriously'. We have completed the first section from creation to Moses' death. We have travelled a long way, not just as far as history and geography are concerned but also spiritually. This guide is only of value if you go back now and dip into these five books and find out for yourself their riches and relevance, and then work them out in your life day by day.

The History

We now turn to the twelve books from Joshua to Esther. These books appear in different places in the Hebrew arrangement. The double volumes appear as single volumes, as does Ezra/Nehemiah. Joshua, Judges, Samuel and Kings are listed as former prophets and Ruth as one of the five rolls read at Pentecost, and Ezra/Nehemiah and Chronicles are put under the latter writings

In other words none of these books appears to be history as we understand it – academic, objective, balanced and detached. We could call these books 'political theology', for there is in all of them a continuous tension between authority and anarchy. Underneath we can hear the cry for a king.

Some of these books were called the 'former prophets', not because they talk about prophets or were written by prophets, but because God revealed himself in action as well as words. These books help us understand God's ways with people.

First is Joshua. It takes up the story from the huge gap caused by the death of Moses. Under his leadership the people had left Egypt and travelled through the wilderness. Now, on the edge of the Promised Land, Moses has died. You can almost sense the uncertainty throughout the camp. Clear leadership is needed to restore confidence. God calls Joshua to stand up and be counted. He faces the loneliness of leadership. Yet leading him would be the commander of the army of the Lord.

6. Joshua –
entering the land – possession

Chapters 1–12 Conquest

a) Entering the land (1–5)
b) Overcoming the land (6–12)
    – centre: Jericho and Ai (6–7)
    – south: Beth Horon (8–10)
    – north: waters of Maron (11)
    – review (12)

Chapters 13–22 Occupation and settlement

– doomsday book of the conquest of Canaan

Chapters 23–24 Two final sermons

– choose this day whom you will serve

The book itself divides in two, in both content and tone. The well-known part is the first section (and the final chapter). The first part deals with the story of the invasion of Canaan, the famous 'Battle' of Jericho, the subsequent defeat at Ai and how the country was conquered. The second part deals with settlement matters, allocating the land among the twelve tribes and the challenge that remained. Finally, Joshua calls the people to recommit themselves to the purpose of God personally, in families and as tribes. '...choose for yourselves this day whom you will serve... But as for me and my household, we will serve the Lord' (24:15) remains one of the great biblical calls to commitment.

The issues raised by the invasion are huge, and the whole story makes us feel uncomfortable today. The land had been promised by God to Abraham 400 years before. When Joshua and the people arrived, how-ever, there were other inhabitants living there. We face problems throughout this section, as it deals with the reality of politics, war and treaties. We are not asked to approve all that was done. We know this because, within the books themselves, some events are clearly condemned. The big issue that cannot be dodged is that it was God who told Joshua to take the land. Worse, he was told not to spare the people he fought. I want to try and face this problem squarely.

Why invade Canaan?

As Christians we make a lot, correctly, of the fact that God is love. God's love is not indifferent to human behaviour. He made us, and he cares how we live. He hates selfishness and sin, and all that degrades us, hurts others, and distances us from him. He will not stand by indifferent or passive when that occurs. So God declares war against sin and will fight it, in whatever way is necessary to secure its defeat. As the Bible says unapologetically, 'The Lord is a warrior' (Exodus 15:3).

God's anger against sin springs from the love in his heart. For if a person is indifferent to evil they can actually be accused of a lack of love. The problem with us is that our anger is often wrongly directed, excessive, and corrupted by other emotions, which makes it in itself sinful. God, however, can be indignant at what sin does and intolerant of sin, without himself sinning.

> God's love is not indifferent to human behaviour. He made us, and he cares how we live.

Ultimately, sin is judged and conquered on the cross. That is why, alongside the truth 'God is love', we assert that 'God is light'. Judgement is God's 'strange work', his 'alien task' (Isaiah 28:21). God holds us responsible for the choices we make, the actions we take, the lifestyle we adopt, the values we hold and the ambitions we pursue. One day he will call us all to account. As Christians we believe in judgement. While the Last Judgement lies ahead, God has chosen to judge individuals, societies and nations throughout history. He can do that by flood, or plague, or fire, and even, as here and elsewhere, by using other nations as his instruments of judgement.

In Psalm 24:8 the writer speaks of the Lord as 'mighty in battle'. In Revelation 19 the Lord Jesus is described as riding on a white horse. The writer adds, 'Out of his mouth comes a sharp sword with which to strike down the nations' (19:15). History is littered with nations unilaterally claiming God as an ally while they pursue their own agenda. 'Holy wars' such as the so-called Crusades are now seen as shameful episodes in our history.

> Ultimately, sin is judged and conquered on the cross.

Yet from time to time the Lord used nations as his instruments of judgement. These nations in turn were judged for their actions when aggressors. They were not immune from God's righteous anger.

The land was a place of sin

From archaeological discoveries we know that Canaan was a land gone to seed, surrendering to those twin vices of sexual depravity and violence. They even condoned child sacrifice. As so often, idolatry led to immorality. When you lose a clear view of God then soon you will lose a clear understanding of goodness. They worshipped the Baals and Asherah, fertility gods who held out the promise of good harvests and children if the people succumbed to their twisted demands for worship.

Judgement was just

The people living in Canaan were not ignorant of the living God. As well as creation around them and conscience within them, they chose to ignore the warnings of their own history (e.g. the flood; the judgement on Sodom and Gomorrah). They also rejected the testimony of the children of Israel, both through the Patriarchs who had lived among them, and the story of Israel's deliverance from Egypt. Not all missed the warning, for Rahab the prostitute saw and responded and became part of our Lord's family tree – see Matthew 1:5. But the nation had become totally corrupted and contaminated all those who came in contact with them. Hard as it is to say, they were like a cancer which had to be excised. The nation was beyond recall, hardened in their ways, hell-bent on destruction. I struggle myself with what this blanket condemnation means, not least for the children, and have no answers to give though the same problem exists with flood and fire.

Abraham, when promised the land, was told it would be 'not yet', for 'the sin of the Amorites [had] not yet reached its full measure' (Genesis 15:13–16). Now, 400 years later, that cup had filled up and was running over. The time had come. God was not creating a playground for his people but a setting in which they were meant to bless the nations of the world.

Invasion was the instrument

Israel was to purge the nation, and did so under direction and discipline. Invasion began with worship. Clear directives were issued about the expected behaviour of the tribes during the invasion. Stray from these and punishment would result. This happened with Achan's sin at Ai (chapter 7), when he took some of the enemy's spoil for himself.

God has no favourites

As they prepared to invade, so a clear warning was given. God does not overlook sin, by anyone. God's people, who know better, are in fact more accountable when they choose sin over holiness. God will not spoil them. They are not exempt from his judgement. In fact, they compromised with the inhabitants, letting them live on in the land and prove to be a thorn in Israel's side. Attracted by local gods, they fell into idolatry. They married local people, took on their ways and values and forgot their God.

Many questions and problems still remain. The invasion of Canaan still presents a huge stumbling block to many people. In our tolerant society today we have become suspicious of certainties and rightly fear ideological fundamentalism, be it religious or political. Yet a world where evil is never called to account would be deeply flawed.

The time came for the invasion to take place. The men were circumcised as a sign of consecration, for this custom had lapsed. The Passover was celebrated, and an altar of witness set up. There was still the Jordan to get past, but a landslide upriver held back the waters long enough to allow the nation to cross.

> God does not overlook sin, by anyone.

Victory at Jericho was followed by a preliminary defeat at Ai, before disobedience was dealt with and victory secured. They left the river basin and travelled up into the hill country. Joshua's military tactics were masterly. He made a central bridgehead, dividing the nation. Then he turned south to confront a confederacy of rival kings at Beth Horon. They were threatening the Gibeonites, who, through a ruse, allied themselves with Joshua. Joshua's troops did not rest on their laurels but in a blitzkrieg operation swept through to the coast, taking on the Philistines, bitter rivals for generations to come. They did not possess the land they had conquered but successfully destroyed the southern power base. They turned north for the third phase of their campaign and met the opposing forces who had rallied together at the Waters of Meron. They were better equipped with chariots but again were defeated by Joshua.

In seven years they secured possession of the land. Now the tribes had to be allocated the work of securing the land. They were apportioned parts in which to settle. Two and half tribes (Reuben, Gad and half of Manasseh) who had fought with Joshua had been promised territory on

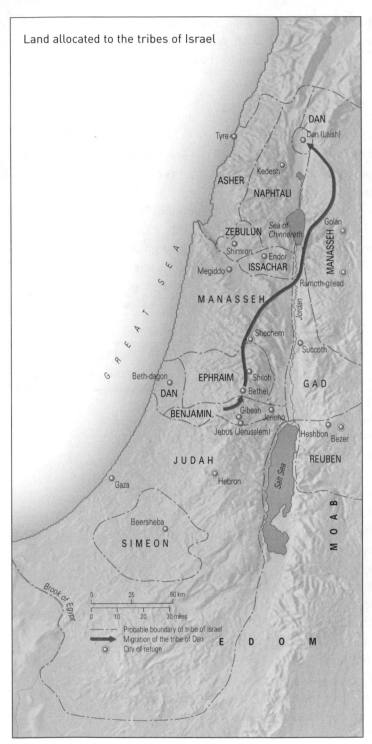

Land allocated to the tribes of Israel

Tyre
DAN
Dan (Laish)
Kedesh
ASHER
NAPHTALI
ZEBULUN
Sea of Chinnereth
Shimron
Endor
Megiddo
ISSACHAR
Golan
MANASSEH
Ramoth-gilead
MANASSEH
Jordan
Shechem
Succoth
Beth-dagon
EPHRAIM
Shiloh
GAD
DAN
Bethel
BENJAMIN
Gibeah
Jericho
Jebus (Jerusalem)
Heshbon
Bezer
JUDAH
Salt Sea
REUBEN
Gaza
Hebron
Beersheba
M O A B
SIMEON
Brook of Egypt
G R E A T   S E A

0   25   50 km
0   10   20   30 miles
——— Probable boundary of tribe of Israel
——→ Migration of the tribe of Dan
◎ City of refuge
E   D   O   M

the East Bank of the Jordan. The other nine and a half were given territory in Canaan itself.

The first tribe to be settled was Judah, then Ephraim. Both tribes secured their inheritance. The other tribes were given title deeds but had still to take the land. The second half of the book reads like the *Domesday Book*, describing borders and allocations. But, as Joshua reminded them at the end of the book in one of two great sermons, the challenge remained. The Lord had given you the land, now possess it. Christians too need to secure the inheritance they have been given by Christ. Nothing will happen unless there is a clear commitment to the Lord.

The story of Joshua ends with his death and that of Aaron's son, Eliazar, the high priest. As a final act, Joseph's bones, carried from Egypt, were at last buried in the land of his birth, the land of promise.

7. Judges –
a sad cycle – decline

Chapters 1– 2 Explanation and introduction

– retrospective
– prospective

Chapters 3–16 History – seven cycles

North – Othniel, Deborah and Barak, Gideon
East of Jordan – Ehud, Jephthah
South and west – Shamgar and Samson

Chapters 17–21 Illustrative epilogue

– infidelity (17–18)
– immorality (19–21)

The book of Judges is vaguely known through Sunday-school stories of Gideon and Samson. Like Numbers, it is a sad book of unfulfilled potential. Time and again the nation fails to learn to trust God. Judges begins by recounting the immediate aftermath of Joshua's time. We read again and again, 'This tribe did not drive out the people of the land but allowed them to dwell'. That was the root of their subsequent troubles. You cannot play with fire and expect not to be burned.

The first two chapters describe the cyclical nature of the period and then move on to tell stirring tales of grim oppression and glorious deliverance. But even heroes can have feet of clay. Nothing lasts, everything is temporary, and soon the nation sinks back to familiar depths. The diagram below portrays the recurring cycle:

The shape of Judges

A fourfold movement

a) departure from God
b) defeat by enemies
c) distress of Israel
d) deliverance by God

The people forgot God and turned away from him. Without his protection, they were vulnerable to aggressors. The neighbouring tribes, sensing an opportunity, took advantage. They either made devastating raiding trips, or occupied parts of the land. Life became so miserable that the people eventually cried out to the God of their fathers. Graciously, repeatedly, the Lord raised up deliverers, called judges, to rescue them. Sadly, within years of being delivered, they forgot the Lord, and once again the sad cycle recurred. From north (Mesopotamia), west (Philistines), east (Moab and Ammon) and south they came (Midianites, Amalekites and Edomites). It didn't help that, at this stage (and later), people thought primarily in tribal rather than national terms. Often they left one another to their own misery rather than presenting a united front.

> The people forgot God and turned away from him. Without his protection, they were vulnerable to aggressors.

There are some great stories in Judges that are easy to read. Ehud the left-handed Benjamite – who stabbed obese King Eglon as he sat on the toilet, whereby his folds of fat enveloped the knife – appealed to me as a teenager! Here are the cycles.

Seven cycles of oppression

Oppressor	Duration	Deliverer
Mesopotamia	8 years	Othniel
Eglon, King of Moab (Philistines)	18 years	Ehud, Shamgar
Jabin, king of Canaan and Sisera	20 years	Deborah, Barak and Jael
Midianites	7 years	Gideon
Civil war, Abimelech	3 years	Tola, Jair
Ammonites	18 years	Jephthah
Philistines	40 years	Samson

The Judges

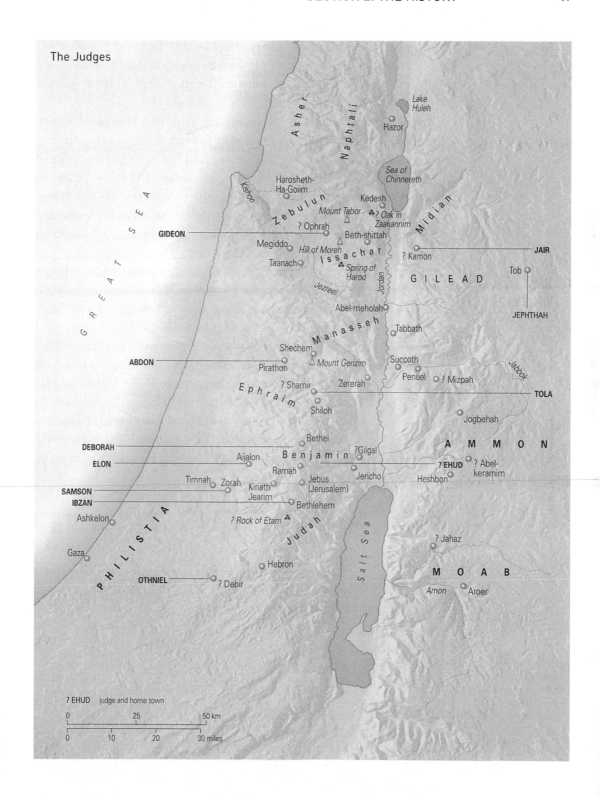

Lake Huleh

Asher

Naphtali

Hazor

Sea of Chinnereth

Harosheth-Ha-Goiim

Kishon

Zebulun

Kedesh

Mount Tabor

? Oak in Zaanannim

Midian

GIDEON ——— ? Ophrah

Beth-shittah

Megiddo

Hill of Moreh

Issachar

? Kamon

JAIR

GILEAD

Tob

Taanach

Spring of Harod

Jezreel

Jordan

Abel-meholah

JEPHTHAH

Manasseh

Tabbath

Shechem

Succoth

ABDON ———

Pirathon

△ Mount Gerizim

Penuel

? Mizpah

Jabbok

Ephraim

? Shamir

Zererah

TOLA

Shiloh

Jogbehah

Bethel

A M M O N

DEBORAH ———

?Gilgal

ELON ———

Aijalon

B e n j a m i n

Ramah

? EHUD

? Abel-keramim

Timnah

Zorah

Jebus (Jerusalem)

Jericho

Heshbon

SAMSON ———

Kiriath Jearim

IBZAN ———

Bethlehem

Ashkelon

? Rock of Etam

Judah

Salt Sea

? Jahaz

Gaza

Hebron

M O A B

OTHNIEL ——— ? Debir

Arnon

Aroer

G R E A T   S E A

P H I L I S T I A

? EHUD   judge and home town

0   25   50 km

0   10   20   30 miles

Dip in and read how Barak was stirred to action by Deborah the prophet-ess, and how the opposing forces (chariots) were rendered useless by a rainstorm. Discover a new use for a tent peg. Sisera at least got the point. Such a thing had not entered his head before!

The Midianites had a secret weapon – camel power. Their desert raid-ing parties were quick and overwhelming. Gideon, dithering around, hid-ing in holes, venturing out at night, tested God not once but twice. Read how sound effects can cause chaos in the ranks of those who like to strike out first and ask questions afterwards. Numbers are not every-thing. But some things he did not learn. Believing his press officials' spin, he led the nation astray in old age. He is not the only leader to let arrogance cloud his judgement. Beware hubris.

Read of Jephthah, the hard man with his macho vows and their tragic consequences. Read of Samson with his raging hormones and ill-disci-plined life. Both delivered the nation, but at a terrible price. God used them, but how much greater they could have been.

The book finishes with two seedy stories showing the depths to which the tribes have sunk. Sordid and depressing, they are best summed up in the telling comment 'Israel had no king. Everyone did as the saw fit' (Judges 21:25). Later that slogan would be rebranded in Corinth as 'All things are lawful', and in the 1960s as 'Do your own thing'. Each is a statement of social and moral anarchy. The ultimate judge is the individ-ual. No one else has a right to comment. Not surprisingly, the damage that follows is considerable.

Effect

a) Cause – religious apostasy – toleration led to admiration led to imita-tion
b) Course – political disintegration
c) Curse – social chaos – immorality, lawlessness

The next book, set in the time of the Judges, provides a refreshing con-trast. It *is* possible to be countercultural. The little book of Ruth is a gem, and, like the story of Rahab, tells of another foreigner in Jesus' family tree.

8. Ruth – faith amid faithlessness – love

Chapters 1–2 The choice of faith

a) Love speaks its mind – resolve (1)
b) Love does its duty – service (2)

Chapter 3 The venture of faith

Love seeks its lover – request

Chapter 4 The reward of faith

Love fulfils its hope – joy

The book of Ruth really forms an appendix to Judges, and is a simple tale of love found at harvest time. The setting is fairly bleak. Failure of the harvest drives a family to emigrate east, seeking a new start. The enterprise is doomed and, despite both sons marrying, no children result. The deaths, first of Naomi's husband, Elimelech, and then of her two sons, Mahlon and Kilion, leave her devastated. It is time to go home, so she releases her daughters-in-law from any sense of obligation to her. Orpah heeds her advice, although genuinely sad to leave her. But Ruth refuses, in memorable words: 'Don't urge me to leave you or to turn back from you. Where you go, I will go, and where you stay I will stay. Your people will be my people and your God my God. Where you die I will die and there will I be buried. May the Lord deal ever so severely if anything but death separates you and me.' Not many would say that about their mother-in-law!

> This is more than how to keep faith in a faithless society.

The story of their return, Ruth's helpfulness, Boaz' interest, Naomi's planning and then the legal obstacles that have to be overcome before its triumphant conclusion all combine to make a good story. This is more than how to keep faith in a faithless society. The final twist comes when we realize that this marriage led, in a few generations, to the birth of one of the greatest figures in the Bible, King David.

9. First Book of Samuel – give us a king – transition

Things are changing in Israel, and not least in the role that the Judges are taking in the land. Men such as Jephthah and Samson were warriors, Eli was primarily a priest, and Samuel stands out as a prophet as well as a judge.

Samuel is the key figure in the transition. The day of the warrior judges has passed. Ruler and priest are being combined in what is being increasingly seen as a hereditary role. We see this in 1 Samuel where Eli, the weak priest, was also called to act as judge.

Once again the pain of childlessness sets the scene for the story. We are reminded of Sarah and of Rachel's pain when we read of Hannah's distress. She is childless while in a polygamous relationship. Elkanah's love cannot compensate for her distress, which is made worse by her rival Peninnah's gloating. Desperation drives her to God. With little thought of how she appeared (which was drunk!), she poured out her heart to God and offered back any future son, if the Lord granted her request.

Samuel was born and, in a strange childhood, brought up in the male society of the altar at Shiloh, with its elderly priest and his arrogant and wicked sons for company. These sons not only blasphemed against God by misappropriating sacrifices, but were also guilty of flagrant immorality. Into this unpromising situation God moved, raising up Samuel, last of the Judges, who would dominate life in the nation for fifty years. He would usher in two profound changes, the institution of the monarchy and the founding of the school of the prophets. The king would unite the tribes into a nation, and the prophet would remind the king that he was answerable to the Lord.

Chapters 1–7 Last of the Judges – Eli and Samuel

'Ichabod' – the glory has departed

Chapters 8–15 First of the Kings – Samuel and Saul

'I have played the fool'– a king is asked for

Chapters 16–31 Preparation of God's anointed – Saul and David

'The man after God's own heart'– a king is given

Samuel is involved in the coronation of the first two kings of Israel, who would each reign for about forty years. The people were not impressed by the behaviour of Eli's sons, nor of Samuel's. More seriously, they were not convinced, after military defeat, of the Lord's power to defend them. It had been more religious superstition than faith that had caused them to take the ark into battle, where they had witnessed not only defeat but also the capture of the ark. The nation was at its lowest ebb – Ichabod: the glory had departed.

When the people asked Samuel for a king it was not just because of his sons' failure. Rather, they wanted to be like all the other nations. Yet they were meant to be 'unlike all the nations', for the Lord was their king. So it was the Lord's leadership they were rejecting, preferring style over substance and image over reality.

The Lord reluctantly granted the people their request but warned them clearly what a monarchy would mean in terms of taxes, conscription and division between rich and poor. People hear only what they want to hear. They saw only how a king would unite their tribes, making them a force to be reckoned with, and so they pressed home their request.

So Samuel gave them what they wanted – a king like all the other nations. Saul was outwardly impressive and a brave fighter, but inwardly weak. That weakness would destroy him in the end. To counterbalance the king's absolute power, God raised up prophets, who would speak God's words to the king and the people.

The first book of Samuel falls into three parts, each centred on a key relationship – Eli and Samuel, Samuel and Saul and then Saul and David. The two books of Samuel tell a powerful tale of power and politics, faith and disobedience, friendship and betrayal. This is the stuff of newspapers – power, politics and personalities, courtroom battles and bedroom antics. It is all the more fascinating because of the unseen but constant presence of God, whether acknowledged or resisted.

Saul started well, but self-will and disobedience robbed him of his mandate. Like Aaron with the golden calf, he put expediency before integrity. Samuel told him that, by so doing, he was rejected by God. He became increasingly paranoid, lashing out at others when the demons were within him. In the process, through jealousy and later suspicion, he alienated his key commander, David, and lost the heart but not the loyalty of his son, Jonathan. No wonder that, towards the end, Saul would say, 'I have played the fool', and so he had.

> The two books of Samuel tell a powerful tale of power and politics, faith and disobedience, friendship and betrayal.

What a contrast David provides. He was a person after God's own heart. His call by Samuel (chapter 16), his victory over Goliath (chapter 17) and his friendship with Jonathan (chapters 19 and 20) have been told and retold by successive generations, as have the accounts of his being hunted and harried by Saul.

The end of the book provides haunting images of the consequences of a life gone wrong. Saul, rejecting God's word, sought out the witches of Endor for counsel. Facing defeat on Mount Gilboa, and with Jonathan dead, he commits suicide.

10. Second Book of Samuel – David's forty-year reign – consecration

Chapters 1–10 David's triumphs

a) King over Judah, Seven years (1–4)
b) King over all Israel, Thirty-three years (5–10)
   – throne established, ark brought (5–7)
   – kingdom extended (8–10)

Chapters 11–24 David's troubles

a) In his family (11–18)
b) In the nation (19–24)

The story continues in 2 Samuel. David's respect for the office of king, shown repeatedly while Saul was alive, continues in his moving eulogy on receiving the news of Saul and Jonathan's deaths. Later he will demonstrate his integrity, in his compassionate dealing with Mephibosheth, Jonathan's son (2 Samuel 9).

This is now David's hour, and he takes on the leadership thirteen years after being anointed. The story of Saul takes up twenty-five chapters, that of David sixty-one. It took seven years for civil war against Ish-Bosheth and his general, Abner, to be won. The decisive move happened when Abner defected. Seeing which way the wind blew, he joined David. That did not please all David's troops. His rival general, Joab (whose brother had been killed by Abner), assassinated him. The precedent of using violence for political ends had been established. Murder, however it is dressed up, is the not the way to solve problems! Ish-Bosheth was, in the end, killed by his own troops. Peace could now come to the land. David was crowned king not only of Judah but of all Israel, a position he held for the next thirty-three years. He moved his capital from Hebron in the south to the politically neutral and strategic Jerusalem, for ever after the city of David.

Jerusalem would become not just the political but also the religious capital. David moved the ark of the covenant into the heart of the city and made preparations to build a temple to house it. David was promised (chapter 7) that he would inaugurate an everlasting kingdom. Too much blood, though, had been spilt by David to allow him to build the Temple. That task would be given to his son, Solomon. The next fifty years would be seen, in retrospect, as the golden years of the monarchy. No super-power threatened them. Through strength of arms they made peace with all their neighbours, ending generations of trouble going back to Joshua's day.

But while so much was going well nationally, problems at home were not difficult to find. The moment of victory was also the hour of defeat. With military matters under control, David stayed at home instead of leading the troops. Enter Bathsheba, and the compelling drama unfolded that centred on the 'set up' of Uriah, her husband – marked out for death. David's action put his reputation into the hands of the unscrupulous Joab, which was not a wise thing to do. Adultery, murder, deceit – one act led to another just because David couldn't control his hormones! He was not the last leader for whom power was an aphro-disiac, and who believed he was beyond the law. His exposure by Nathan – 'You are the man!' – cut through the web of self-deceit David had established, bringing him crashing down to earth. David's calibre is seen by his genuine repentance.

But saying sorry doesn't undo the consequences of sin. His child by Bathsheba died and his family, increasingly lacking moral leadership, ran wild. Amnon raped his half-sister, Tamar. Absalom, her brother, killed Amnon and was exiled. Absalom was restored but aspired to the throne and rebelled against David, who had to flee. Joab, the fixer, killed Absalom against the king's orders. David's distress at the death of his son provides a haunting anticipation of the cross: 'O my son Absalom! My son, my son Absalom! If only I had died instead of you – O Absalom, my son, my son!' Joab, with political capital in his hand, rebuked David for grieving for a rebel, and the monarchy was restored – but at what a cost.

> ... saying sorry doesn't undo the consequences of sin.

The seeds of rebellion proved intoxicating. Others tried their hand at toppling David, but with little success. This was because Joab acted first and asked questions afterwards. These were now uncertain days, with famine and wars as well as rebellion. It was clear that David's great rule had now run its course. There is a certain sadness about the end of

David's reign, often repeated in the lives of great political figures. The book finishes with an appendix about the deeds of David's mighty men and the songs David sang.

Let us take a moment to see where we are in history.

Take the dates 2000 BC , 1000 BC, and 1 AD:

2000 BC Abraham
         Isaac
         Jacob

         Time in Egypt

         Moses
         Wilderness
         Joshua
         Judges

         Saul

1000 BC David
         Solomon

Kingdom of Israel   Kingdom of Judah

722 BC Conquered by Assyrians

         586 Conquered by Babylonians
         536 Zerubbabel and 50,000 return
         516 Temple rebuilt
         458 Ezra
         445 Nehemiah – city walls rebuilt

         400 years' silence

BC/AD Jesus

---

11. First Book of Kings – division of the kingdom – disruption

Chapters 1–12 Kingdom undivided

a) David and Solomon – years of strength
b) The glory and tragedy of Solomon's forty-year reign
   – glory: peace, wisdom, Temple, trade
   – tragedy: extravagance, despotic rule, polygamy, foreign alliances, idolatry, slave labour

Chapters 12–22 Kingdom divided

a) The first eighty years of the two kingdoms – years of struggle
b) The glory and tragedy of Elijah's ministry
   – glory: Carmel – a second Moses
   – tragedy: nation did not turn, nor did throne

The story of 2 Samuel is continued in 1 Kings, though not in quite as racy a style. It tells the story of the last of the kings who ruled over the united kingdom and then alternates between Israel and Judah. The two dominating figures in this book are Solomon at the beginning and Elijah at the end.
   The three marks of Solomon's reign are:

a) **his wisdom** in the judgements he made, the proverbs he collected and the peace and prosperity that prevailed; the widespread trade he encouraged;
b) the construction and dedication of **the Temple**;
c) **his foolishness** in his personal life, his many marriages, his extravagance (e.g. the palace took twice as long to build as the Temple), the cost of the standing army and navy, and the alliances that bound him to other nations and watered down his distinctive faith.

It is worth noting that the period that follows is viewed through four lenses in the Old Testament:

Solomon's Temple

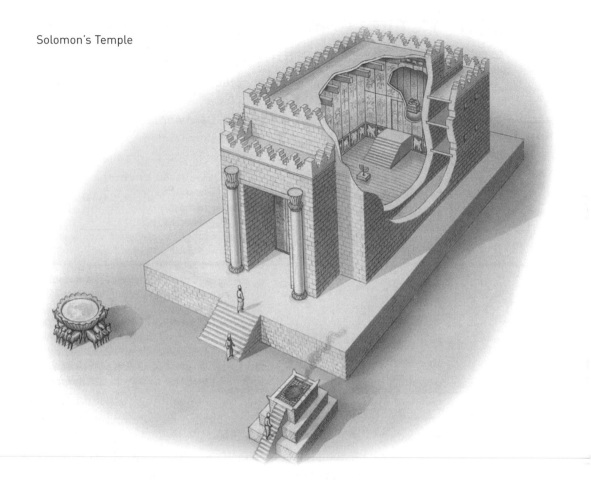

- Samuel and Kings – emphasis on politics
- Chronicles – emphasis on worship
- The Prophets – emphasis on religion and morality
- The Psalms – emphasis on devotion.

The death of Solomon brings a desire for change. Solomon's extensive building programme required conscripted labour and heavy taxes. It is time for new policies. The new king is counselled by the wise to relax his demands, but the young hotheads argue that any concession will be interpreted as weakness and advocate a hard-line strategy. Rehoboam listens to the younger generation, with disastrous consequences.

He sparks a revolution, which divides the kingdom for ever (chapter 12). Only Judah and Benjamin are left with the Levites (who staff the

> Every king did what was evil in the eyes of the Lord. Yet, to this kingdom, God sent at least four outstanding prophets to minister.

Temple), as the ten northern tribes form their own nation, called variously Israel or Ephraim (after the largest tribe in the north), or Samaria (after the new capital built later by King Omri). The rebels needed to establish new centres of worship to replace the Temple. Golden calves were erected at Bethel and Dan: Aaron's foolishness in the wilderness was still causing problems.

The story of the northern kingdom is one of gradual decline and increasing wickedness. Every king did what was evil in the eyes of the Lord. Yet, to this kingdom, God sent at least four outstanding prophets to minister:

1. Elijah – message of judgement
2. Elisha – message of grace
3. Amos – message of judgement
4. Hosea – message of grace.

The south would have mainly weak and wicked kings but there were some outstanding monarchs. Some started well and finished badly (e.g. Uzziah); others who started badly and finished better (e.g. Manasseh). The two most outstanding kings in the south were Hezekiah who prompted a religious revival and Josiah who prompted a spiritual renewal.

It might be helpful to set the kingdoms side by side. 1 Kings tells the story of the two kingdoms during their first eighty years and 2 Kings completes the story.

History of the Kings

All Israel

Saul (reigned forty years)
David (reigned forty years)

——— **1000 BC** ———

Solomon (reigned forty years)

Israel, northern kingdom	Judah, southern kingdom
10 tribes:	2 tribes plus Levi:
capital: Samaria	capital: Jerusalem
19 kings, 9 dynasties	19 kings, 1 queen, 1 dynasty
all bad	mostly bad but some good
	12 bad, 5 good, 2 unstable

Israel	Judah
Jeroboam 1 (22)	Rehoboam (17)
Nadab (2)	Abijah (3)
————	
Baasha (24)	Asa (41)

———— **900 BC** ————

Israel	Judah
Elah (2)	
————	
Zimri (7 days)	
————	
Omri (12)	
Ahab (22)	Jehoshaphat (25)
Ahaziah (2)	**End of 1 Kings**
Joram (12)	Jehoram (8)
————	
Jehu (28)	Ahaziah (1)
	Queen Athaliah (7)
Jehoahaz (17)	Joash (40)

———— **800 BC** ————

Israel	Judah
Jehoash (16)	Amaziah (29)
Jeroboam II (41) (prosperity N and S)	Uzziah (or Azariah) (52)
Zechariah (six months)	
————	
Shallum (one month)	
————	
Menahem (10)	
Pekahiah (2)	
————	
Pekah (20)	Jotham (16)
————	

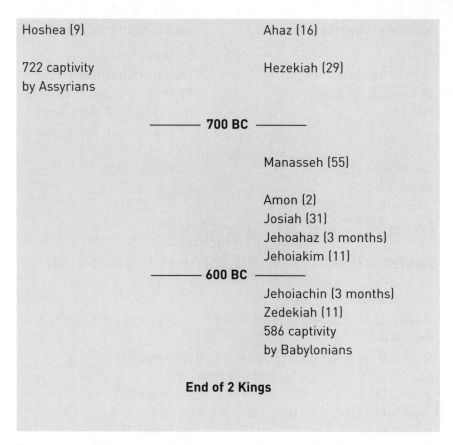

Hoshea (9)   Ahaz (16)

722 captivity   Hezekiah (29)
by Assyrians

——————— **700 BC** ———————

                                    Manasseh (55)

                                    Amon (2)
                                    Josiah (31)
                                    Jehoahaz (3 months)
                                    Jehoiakim (11)
——————— **600 BC** ———————
                                    Jehoiachin (3 months)
                                    Zedekiah (11)
                                    586 captivity
                                    by Babylonians

                      End of 2 Kings

The focus at the end of 1 Kings is on the northern kingdom and the extraordinary ministry of Elijah, confronting King Ahab and his evil queen, Jezebel. Jezebel came from Tyre and brought her gods with her. She actively tried to suppress Israel's religion. Elijah denounced the throne and its false gods and sentenced the nation to drought as a sign of God's displeasure (one of the curses of the covenant). Three years later, as drought devastated the land, he met Ahab face to face and called for a showdown. It was high noon. The confrontation on Mount Carmel is a hinge moment for the nation, with Elijah's question (1 Kings 18:21) echoing Joshua's challenge and anticipating Jesus' choices in the Sermon on the Mount. 'How long', asked Elijah, 'will you waver between two opinions? If the Lord is God, follow him; but if Baal is God, follow him.' The triumph of Carmel is followed by a vivid tale of flight and depression in the wilderness. Five years later, the confrontation in Naboth's vineyard set a clock running that would, in time, seal Ahab and Jezebel's fate and that of their family.

Despite the miraculous signs, the nation was not for turning. Miracles in the Bible largely occur in four periods and otherwise are very rare indeed:

- the period of Moses and the exodus
- the period of Elijah and Elisha
- the period of Daniel and the exile
- the period of Jesus and the New Testament church.

12. Second Book of Kings – downfall of the kingdoms – dispersion

Chapters 1–10 Annals of Israel, the northern kingdom

– the ministry of Elisha – years of struggle

Chapters 11–17 Alternating annals of both kingdoms

the fall of Israel to the Assyrians – years of storm

Chapters 18–25 Annals of Judah, the southern kingdom, a single kingdom

– the fall of Judah to the Babylonians – sunset years

The second book of Kings tells the story from corruption to captivity. The story of Elijah finishes with him being taken to heaven. Later, the story of Judah ends with the nation being taken to Babylon.

Elisha had been Elijah's apprentice during the closing years of his ministry. He became heir to his cloak and his calling, though his ministry was distinctly different.

The contrasting ministry of Elijah and Elisha

Elijah	Elisha
solitary	social
desert	court
to nation	to remnant
judgement	grace

In 2 Kings, we move between north and south. Whereas the line of Judah in the south remains unbroken, there are nine different dynasties in the north. The nation tumbles into disorder and disintegration, resisting the pleas of the prophets. Eventually the northern kingdom is overrun by the superpower, Assyria, whose capital was Nineveh. Judah, led by King Hezekiah supported by the prophet Isaiah, was miraculously delivered from Sennacherib (perhaps by a plague in the enemy camp – 185,000 died overnight). They survived for another 130-plus years before they too, first by deportation and then by destruction, were overrun by the Babylonians, the next superpower to arise.

Whereas the Assyrian policy was to assimilate conquered people so that they lost any sense of national identity, Babylon allowed its conquered peoples a degree of freedom. People could keep their own ways, traditions and beliefs. So Judah could return to the Promised Land while the other ten tribes (except for a dedicated few) disappeared for ever. The remnants of Israel who were left in their land married incoming settlers, and out of that mix the Samaritans emerged. They took the Torah alone as their scripture.

Later they opposed Nehemiah when he tried to rebuild the walls of Jerusalem.

Then they built their own temple on Mount Gerazim, which the Jews destroyed when the Samaritans opposed their war of independence under the Maccabees in the second century BC. There was, therefore, a history of hostility between the Jews and the Samaritans, which is reflected in the radical teaching and ministry of Jesus in John 4 and Luke 10 and 17.

The fall of Babylon in three stages

- 606 BC First deportation of youth (Daniel and other prime candidates for indoctrination)

- 597 Second deportation (10,000) (Ezekiel and Mordecai [uncle of Esther])
- 586 Third deportation of the rest (city and Temple destroyed, king taken into captivity)

> The nation tumbles into disorder and disintegration, resisting the pleas of the prophets.

When we come to Chronicles there is a different feel and perspective. We cover the same period as in 1 and 2 Kings but from a different angle.

Samuel/ Kings	Chronicles
personal and biographical	statistical and official
simple, faithful records of what happened	selective extracts for a purpose
Judah and Israel	Judah only – line of promise David's house
political and royal	religious

Different perspectives

You can see how this works out when you look at an outline. Chronicles is listed as one of the latter writings, along with its companion volume and the two that follow it, Ezra/Nehemiah.

13. First Book of Chronicles – the house of the Lord – worship

Chapters 1–9   Israel's main genealogies – its people

a) Primeval and patriarchal (1)
b) National – the chosen (2–9)

Chapters 10–29   David's reign – its preparation

a) The anointed of the Lord (10–12)
   – Saul (10)
   – David (11 onwards)
b) The ark of the Lord (13–16)
c) The covenant of the Lord (17–21)
d) The Temple of the Lord (22–28)

One reason why Chronicles is not a gripping read is that it draws from at least fourteen different sources, including many official records with statistics and genealogies. In Samuel and Kings the story carries the major focus. The personalities are instantly recognizable.

At first sight there is little warmth or glow to the books of Chronicles. They appear austere and cold. But we mustn't rush past them, because they are compiled for a purpose. The editor is not interested in the rebel northern kingdom, which is regarded as an apostate nation, beyond redemption. Politics and personalities are of no lasting interest. The chroniclers look back from beyond the monarchy and exile to help re-establish their national identity and secure their religious heritage. What matters is who they are, where they have come from, and what they are called to do.

Supremely, they are called to worship and serve God. Kings have come and gone and no voice from a prophet is heard, so the mantle of custodians of the faith falls on the priests. Their base is the Temple. They want to encourage loyalty to God. You cannot live life with no reference to God without dire consequences.

The difference between the prophetic and the priestly standpoint

Prophetic standpoint	**Priestly standpoint**
Exposes people's guilt	Encourages loyalty to God

Much fun has been made of the endless 'begat' chapters that comprise 1 Chronicles (chapters 1–9). Yet people matter. Individuals have names, stories and personalities. Working together for God can make a difference. Here is a story of history, unbroken through the generations; a story of vision held by faithful men and women from Adam throughout the history of Israel, beyond destruction to their return under Zerubbabel, and later Ezra and Nehemiah.

Amid the many names there is a thin line of promise:

- Adam
- Seth
- Noah
- Shem
- Abraham
- Isaac
- Jacob
- Judah
- Rahab
- Ruth
- David
- Solomon
- Kings of Judah down to the captivity.

> The chroniclers look back from beyond the monarchy and exile to help re-establish their national identity and secure their religious heritage.

We notice that God, ignoring natural descent, chooses those lives that will demonstrate faith and obedience. Disobedience and unbelief disqualify people from his purposes. So Abraham is chosen, and, in time, David.

For the writer, what matters about David is everything that takes place after he is crowned king, and it comes under four headings:

1) As the anointed of the Lord, Bethlehem, his birthplace, will one day become centre stage and have its fifteen minutes of fame

2) The ark, signifying the centrality of worship, is brought to the new capital, Jerusalem, and placed at the centre of their national life
3) The covenant, God's promise, is renewed with David and has a future focus: 'your throne will have no end'
4) Preparations for the Temple will be his legacy, to be completed by Solomon.

These are the lasting legacies of David's reign. The Bible does not teach of a church being established by a nation but of a nation being established by a church.

14. Second Book of Chronicles – Temple versus throne – apostasy

Chapters 1–9 The reign of Solomon

a) The Temple built – seven years
b) The throne magnified – fourteen years

Chapters 10–36 The kings of Judah

a) The Temple destroyed
b) The throne captured

> The second book of Chronicles is a warning of how fast a nation and a church can decline.

Again, the sad tale is told of the downfall of the southern kingdom. Not only were the majority of kings on the throne wicked, but even the Temple, meant to preserve and encourage spiritual vigour, actually contributed to the decline. It was too easy for worship to move from heart to lips, for reality to be replaced by ritualism. When that happened, the Temple, far from promoting spiritual life, paralysed it. Worse, it poisoned the minds and hearts of the people until they turned away from the living God.

Furthermore, the hope of king and priest working together, as exemplified by David, ended up with 'throne versus Temple' as each tussled for power, to their mutual destruction.

The writer of 2 Chronicles passes over more dubious aspects of Solomon's legacy to focus on his enduring contribution, the completion and dedication of the Temple. The story thereafter is one of spiralling decline, which cannot be halted even by good kings and great prophets. The two outstanding kings of Judah were undoubtedly Hezekiah and Josiah. The great prophets included Isaiah, his contemporary Micah, and Jeremiah and his contemporaries Habakkuk and Zephaniah. As Hezekiah depended on Isaiah so Josiah drew strength and wisdom from Jeremiah.

The second book of Chronicles is a warning of how fast a nation and a church can decline. The people were led off in chains to Babylon 135 years after Hezekiah and Isaiah had seen off the Assyrian menace. Their Temple had been destroyed and their city lay in ruins. Let him who thinks he stands take care, lest he fall.

The nation was systematically dismantled in three stages but the end result was exile and disaster. Even those who had been taken into exile in the first two phases did not believe it was possible for Jerusalem or the Temple to fall. No matter what Jeremiah said to the people in Jerusalem, or what Ezekiel prophesied to the exiles in Babylon, neither group were prepared for the total destruction that followed. Tragically for some, their faith went also. Yet God had warned that those not worthy of living in the land would be vomited out, and so it happened. But with the exile came a purging. Israel went into exile as a nation and returned as a church. An incurably idolatrous nation returned as the most monotheistic nation in the world. So traumatic had been the experience of exile, with its suffering and difficulties, that their desire to go after foreign gods was dealt with, once and for all.

The final three books of history (in a peculiar parallel to the final three books of prophecy, Haggai, Zechariah and Malachi) deal with events in the period after the fall of Jerusalem. The fall itself is enshrined in the book of Lamentations, read at the anniversary of the destruction each year.

The first of these books is Ezra, followed by its companion volume, Nehemiah. They tell of the three phases of the return from exile to Jerusalem.

We can set out these three phases as follows:

Return from Babylon

1) 539 BC Babylon falls to Persians
    536 BC Cyrus, King of Persia, allows 50,000 to return. Zerubbabel leads the return
    516 BC Temple rebuilt
2) 458 BC Ezra (Esther in Susa)
3) 445 BC Nehemiah – city walls rebuilt

After the time prophesied by Jeremiah (seventy years) (Jeremiah 25:11, 12; 29:10, 11), there was a change of government. The Babylonians were overthrown by the Persians. Cyrus the king is one of the most significant figures in secular history. In historical terms he ranks with Alexander the Great. In twelve years he was to destroy three empires. He ushered in a period of Persian superiority that lasted for 200 years. Yet, fascinatingly, God used this pagan ruler, who had no thought of the Lord, as his instrument to fulfil his purposes for his people. Isaiah dares to call Cyrus 'the Lord's anointed', meaning not God's ultimate messiah, but one whom God would use to carry forward his plans.

With the change of rule came a new foreign policy. Cyrus, having overthrown Belshazzar on the night of the famous feast recorded in Daniel chapter 5 and taken control of the vast empire, allowed the Jews to return to their homeland. He decided that the stability of the empire would be better served if the peoples within it were allowed to return to their own lands and worship their own gods. For most of the exiles their time away was only fifty years (not seventy). This was because twenty years of Babylonian rule had taken place before the final destruction of Jerusalem forced the majority into exile. However, even that was too long for many Jews to contemplate return. They had lived all their lives in Babylon, settled down, had families and found work. They were reluctant to return to the wreckage of their national past. Life in exile had proved acceptable. Only 50,000 were prepared to make the long journey back across the desert, led by Zerubbabel. Most of them were second-generation exiles.

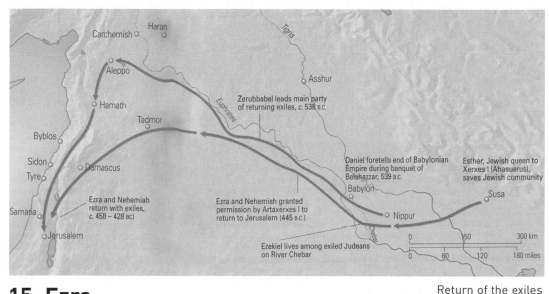

Return of the exiles

15. Ezra –
a returning remnant – reconstruction

Chapters 1–6 Return under Zerubbabel the prince

following the decree of Cyrus
a) Return (1–2)
b) Reorganization (3–6) – Temple dedicated

Chapters 7–10 Return under Ezra the scribe

following the decree of Artaxerxes (sixty years later)
a) Return (7–8)
b) Reformation (9–20) – people consecrated

The book of Ezra deals with two waves of the returning remnant. We can easily miss the sixty-year gap between the end of chapter 6 and the beginning of chapter 7. It is likely that the story of Esther is set during that gap of sixty years. Without Esther's courage there might not have been an Ezra to lead the people back!

The first remnant to return was led by Zerubbabel. Zerubbabel was of the royal line of David, for although the throne was toppled the royal line had continued. It would continue underground until a carpenter of royal blood was betrothed to a teenage girl, also of royal blood, and a baby called Jesus was born in David's birthplace, Bethlehem.

Working with Zerubbabel was Joshua the priest. For those pioneers the challenge was clear. They had to go back to a wrecked city, broken walls and a destroyed Temple, and start all over again. Most of those who returned were from the tribe of Judah, but there were a few from the other tribes who had kept their faith and never lost sight of the calling of God on their lives.

> The first thing they did on their return was to build an altar and offer a sacrifice of thanksgiving and dedication to God. They were clear about their priorities.

The first thing they did on their return was to build an altar and offer a sacrifice of thanksgiving and dedication to God. They were clear about their priorities. The first building task was to rebuild the Temple, though not on its previous scale or with its former magnificence. They wanted the Lord to be central and were determined to learn from their past.

Their return created hostility among those living in the land, especially the Samaritans, a mixed-race people with a hybrid faith. Their initial approach offering cooperation was rejected, and attitudes hardened. The Jews (from Judah) were determined to retain their distinctive identity. (It is only now that we are entitled to call them Jews.) Various attempts followed to discourage and hamper the work.

Finally, the Samaritans complained to the new king, Artaxerxes, in his capital at Susa, that the Jews sought independence and that history had shown them to be proven troublemakers. They won their case. Work on the Temple halted for twenty years until King Darius came to the throne. Even then, it took the motivational ministries of the prophets Haggai and Zechariah to galvanize the people to complete the task. Darius, when appealed to, supported the intention of Cyrus and allowed the project to be completed. The new Temple was dedicated with great joy, despite its limitations. The Passover was then celebrated for the first time for many years.

Sixty years pass from that first return, before Ezra comes to Jerusalem. He may have been Secretary of State for Jewish affairs (521–486). He brought reinforcements on the long four- to five-month journey. Though a good start had been made, much remained to be done and there was a need for reformation. The people were intermarrying with the surrounding peoples and losing their vision. He called them back to God. In an act of confession, the people returned to faith.

Ezra was a priest and scribe. His leadership marks the rise to prominence of both scribes and priests for the next 400 years. He also features in the companion volume of Nehemiah, a great story, which is easy to read and obvious in its applications. The writing is lively and full of drama.

16. Nehemiah – rebuilding the walls – reconstruction

Chapters 1–7 The walls rebuilt

– construction in the face of opposition

Chapters 8–10 The Law read

– revival through instruction

Chapters 11–13 The work consolidated

– settlement and reformation

Nehemiah, a civil servant in Susa, whose heart was in Jerusalem, sought news from his homeland. What he heard drove him to prayer and action. The Temple had been rebuilt, but the city remained a disgrace. Ruined walls bore testimony to its sad history, and further damage had been caused by generations using their stones to rebuild their own homes. Organized and purposeful, Nehemiah cares, prays and formulates a clear plan of action. The logistical problems are anticipated and dealt with. With the right bits of paper (he was a civil servant!) and adequate resources, and following proper reconnaissance, he gathers the people and calls them to build up the walls. In a story of

> Organized and purposeful, Nehemiah cares, prays and formulates a clear plan of action.

triumph against opposition, both external threats and internal conflicts follow, which parallel both the early chapters of Acts and much of church life.

There is a lovely moment that shows the clarity and simplicity of Nehemiah's focus. When those opposed to his plans seek to distract him, he says, 'I am doing a great work; why should I stop and come down?'

The walls were rebuilt in fifty-two days! After the building comes the dedication. God's word is read and explained by Ezra, a great prayer is recorded and the Feast of Tabernacles is celebrated. (Interestingly, three great prayers are found in Ezra chapter 9, Nehemiah chapter 9 and Daniel chapter 9). The work, after further reformation by Nehemiah, is secured for another generation. But the lesson of these two books remains that 'the price of freedom is eternal vigilance'.

The last of the historical books, Esther, is a fascinating one because God's name is not mentioned once. Yet his unseen hand dominates throughout. The absence of his name may be because the story is culled from Persian records. Scholars have suggested that God's name is hidden as an acrostic four times in this book. An old hymn, 'Workman of God, O lose not heart', puts it this way:

> Thrice blest is he to whom is given,
> The instinct that can tell
> That God is on the field when he
> Is most invisible!
>
> F.W. Faber

17. Esther – God in the shadows – providence

Chapters 1–4 The grave danger to the Jews

– crisis anticipated

Chapters 5–10 The great deliverance of the Jews

– crisis overruled

God is no showman. He does not need to display himself for our applause or attention. Esther is set in the time of Ahasuerus (or Xerxes) I, who ruled from 486– 465 BC. It starts with an example of the problems caused when people drink too much. The result is a broken marriage and a beauty contest for a new queen. Esther is chosen. She will play a key part in thwarting a plan by the king's prime minister, Haman, an Amalekite, to organize a genocide of the Jews. He harbours a deep hatred for them as a result of a perceived personal slur by Esther's uncle, Mordecai.

Esther alone can save them, but she will have to risk her life to do so. Mordecai challenges her (Esther 4:14): '... if you remain silent at this time, relief and deliverance for the Jews will arise from another place, but you and your father's family will perish. And who knows but that you have come to royal position for such a time as this?' (NIV). Her response is magnificent. Calling on the Jews to fast and pray, she says, 'I will go to the king even though it is against the law. And if I perish, I perish.'

So what happens? Read it, and find out what a wonderful story it is. The events are remembered annually at the Feast of Purim in the Jewish calendar, a living testimony of its historical accuracy. With Esther the seventeen historical books conclude.

The first five books dealt with preparing to enter the land, the next nine deal with what happened when they occupied it, and the final three are concerned with what follows their dispossession.

> God is no showman. He does not need to display himself for our applause or attention.

Section 3

Wisdom Literature

We now move to the second main section of the Old Testament. We have travelled through the books of history and grasped the overall framework of the story. There are a few more stories later on in Daniel 1–6, in Jonah and in odd chapters in some of the longer prophecies, e.g. Isaiah 36–39. Some fill in details of stories we have already looked at. Basically, though, if we master the first seventeen books we have the big picture of the Old Testament.

Now we move to the wisdom literature, in particular to five books in the middle of the Old Testament. There is other wisdom literature, but most of it is concentrated here.

The relationship of the historical books to the writings	
History	**Writings**
historical	experiential
national	personal
story of the Hebrew race	story of the human heart
mainly prose	mainly poetry

In the Old Testament the 'wise man' played a recognized role. Jeremiah writes in Jeremiah 18:18: 'For the teaching of the law by the priest, will not cease, nor will counsel from the wise, nor the word from the prophets.'

Each of these key roles had a human model, though all were flawed:

- Aaron – model of the priest
- Moses – model of the prophet
- David – model of the king
- Solomon – model of the wise man.

> The 'wise man' observes life and reflects on his experience. These five books cover a whole field of human experience.

The 'wise man' observes life and reflects on his experience. These five books cover a whole field of human experience.

Wisdom

- *Job* – where the pain of suffering is transformed by a vision of God the creator
- *Psalms* – reflect on life in God's presence, as it is, without pretence
- *Proverbs* – help us to think through the choices we face in a complex world
- *Ecclesiastes* – encourages us to get out of our ghetto and see the big picture
- *Song of Songs* – shows how the power of sexuality needs to be faced and harnessed.

With a different type of literature we need a different approach. Today we face information overkill but suffer from a shortage of wisdom. People who are wise have mastered the art of living. Christ is the supreme example of how to live, and Paul speaks of Christ as our wisdom (1 Corinthians 1:30). Wisdom is a way of seeing, deciding and acting that leads to life.

To find wisdom you must take God seriously. He must be kept centre stage. As Proverbs 1:7 says, 'The fear of the Lord is the beginning of knowledge'. Wise people, as they observed life, reflected on what they saw, heard and experienced. They often wrote in a poetic form to touch feelings as well as minds. It is important to catch the thrust of what is written, rather than getting bogged down in the details. Images are used and pictures painted, not for us to analyse but to make an impression. These books address our imagination, giving us new insight. Wisdom flourished in days of peace, and supremely in the golden age of David and Solomon.

Let us look then at these five books, one by one.

> To find wisdom you must take God seriously. He must be kept centre stage.

18. Job –
problem of pain – testing –
know yourself

Chapters 1–2 Prologue, prose – Job's disasters

- controversy between God and Satan
- two meetings, though note that evil is under God's hand

Chapters 3–42 Dialogue, poetic drama – Job's debates

a) Job and his friends – Eliphaz, Bildad, Zophar
   – first cycle (4–14)
   – second cycle (15–21)
   – third cycle (22–31)
b) Intervention of Elihu (32–37)
c) Revelation of the Lord (38–42)

Chapter 42 Epilogue, prose – Job's deliverance

- resolution of the controversy
  – Satan routed
  – friends rebuked
  – Job rewarded

The first book of wisdom is Job. Called the oldest story in the world, it may be a real story told in dramatic form. There are references to Job in Ezekiel 14:14 and James 5:11. It is poetic and stylized and written more like one of Shakespeare's 'historical' plays than as a history, giving us the inside story. It is important to read the whole book through and not just dip in (and it is not short!) to get its message, because much of what is said is recorded in order to be refuted! For although the Bible is the word of God we do not claim that God endorses everything it says, or all that happens. It is all God's word; it is not all God's truth. That is why we need to read verses in context. As the saying goes, a verse without a context is a pretext.

The great poetic drama of Job begins with a scene-setter, revealed to us but hidden from Job and his 'comforters'. Satan asserts that Job trusts God only because everything is going well. Remove the props and the edifice will fall. The story tests out Satan's hypothesis by showing how Job responds. Can you go on believing in God when everything is going wrong? Or, more simply, how much *do* you trust God?

> ... although the Bible is the word of God we do not claim that God endorses everything it says, or all that happens. It is all God's word; it is not all God's truth.

For Job the story begins when blessings are replaced with disaster. He struggles to understand what is happening. He has lost everything. News pours in, each bit worse than the last. He has lost his wealth, his family, his standing and his health. Even his wife distances herself from him. He is not totally abandoned, however, for his friends come to him. The best thing they do is to sit with him and say nothing for a week! It is when they open their mouths that the trouble begins. When they speak they go wrong because they remain detached from the problem. Their answers lack intimacy and are reduced to quick-fix solutions. They are sitting beside Job but they do not enter into his situation.

Much of the book is taken up with the speeches of Job's friends and his responses. Each of them speaks in a way that reveals their character, but all of them believe, however it is dressed up, that 'suffering is a judgement on sin'. It is the childhood belief that if you do wrong you will be punished. Job is suffering, so he must have done something wrong. He would not be the last person to have a secret life at odds with to his public image. Job, however, while never thinking of himself as perfect, knows he has no such double life. What you see is what you get. Their standard explanations do not fit the facts. They mistake a proverb 'If you sin you suffer' (which is generally true) for a promise (which is always true). This is even less true in reverse (if you suffer you must have sinned)!

The style and spirit of the three friends is outlined below. Their case makes sense to them, but in fact they are all wrong.

Job's comforters

1) His three friends: 'Suffering is a judgement on sin'
   – God is a judge

   a) Eliphaz:
      – wise, sympathetic, reasoned from experience
      – speaks of God's transcendence

   b) Bildad:
      – forthright, severe, illustrated from history
      – speaks of God's omnipotence

   c) Zophar:
      – dogmatic, bigoted, voice of orthodoxy
      – speaks of God's omniscience

All (including Job) are ignorant of chapters 1–2

2) The fourth friend: 'Suffering is educational'
   – God is a teacher

   d) Elihu: spoke as a brother, *not* as a judge

3) The Lord: 'Suffering calls for self-surrender'.

After three cycles of speeches a fourth friend, Elihu, joins them and gives a different slant. His thesis is that 'suffering is educational'. Suffering cannot be understood simply in terms of retribution – you get what is coming to you. God also uses suffering to teach and build us up. This too, however, doesn't ring true with Job. Eventually the 'friends' are reduced to silence, convinced of Job's intransigence rather than of their defective theology.

As for Job, his suffering is real and not academic. He experiences pain from every direction: economic, social, physical and mental but, supremely, spiritual. He doesn't curse God, as his wife advocates, but he does challenge God.

Then God reveals himself in a majestic and overwhelming way which

> ... God reveals himself in a majestic and overwhelming way which puts them all in their place and puts the problem into perspective.

puts them all in their place and puts the problem into perspective. God is not just like them but larger. He is the mighty God, creator of the heavens and the earth. He is not someone you put in the dock! His interrogation of Job exposes the limitations of our knowledge and understanding. Job's questioning ceases before God's greatness, which is laced with humour, as he speaks of the hippo and the crocodile. What matters to Job is that they are talking again. The blessings that follow are wonderful, but secondary to that truth.

So many lessons emerge from this book. God cares more about our faith than our pleasure, and will risk misunderstanding. One person's faith can make a difference, way beyond anything they can imagine. We will all be tested by the experience of suffering at some point.

Job never finds the solution, but he loses his problem. God does not tell us everything. He tells us enough, however, for us to trust him for the rest and leave room for faith to grow. Job realized that suffering is only

> God cares more about our faith than our pleasure, and will risk misunderstanding.

one part of human experience, not explained by God and not fully understood by us. That is why silence speaks volumes in ministry to those who are suffering. Beyond that, nothing is so relevant as the mystery of the cross on which God's only Son died for us.

19. Psalms –
praise and prayer – hymnbook –
know the Lord

The second book of Wisdom is the Psalms – the Bible's hymn book. The Jews know it as a book of praise and prayer (NB: 'Jew' from 'Judah' means 'praise'.) It is still used today by the church and by individuals to nurture and express faith. It has lasted through the years because it faithfully reflects the huge range of moods in which people come into God's presence. Faith and doubt, fear and hope, anger and trust all walk together in these pages. There is an openness and an honesty that invite the same response from us.

The book of Psalms carries its own divisions, and the five sections may parallel the five books of the Torah. Perhaps they are this way to remind us to listen to God first before we respond. All the psalms speak of God.

Book 1: 1–41 God our saviour

– to be trusted by faith

Book 2: 42–72 God our king

– to be obeyed as we submit to him

Book 3: 73–89 God our guide

– to be appealed to in hope

Book 4: 90–106 God the eternal

– to be worshipped and loved

Book 5: 107–150 God the wonder-worker

– to be praised with joy

Psalms is the largest book in the Bible and the easiest to find, being in the middle. Speaking to the heart and the universal human condition, it requires the least translation from one culture to another. Even the lines of poetry reflect parallel ideas (which can be translated) rather than rhythm or rhyme (which can't). The psalms were written over a period of 1,000 years beginning at least 2,500 years ago, yet they are still fresh today.

In this book are 150 songs that can be said, sung or

> [Psalms] faithfully reflects the huge range of moods in which people come into God's presence. Faith and doubt, fear and hope, anger and trust all walk together in these pages.

shouted, in private or in public. Some are 'I, me' psalms; others are 'we, our'. Worship is a corporate as well as a personal experience. We use the psalms for worship, for prayer and for life. Psalms is the most quoted book in New Testament. The most-quoted verse is Psalm 110:1. Of 283 citations of the Old Testament in the New Testament, 116 come from the psalms. There are also other psalms, for example those found in Exodus 15, Jonah 2, and Lamentations.

The psalms vary in length (from 2 to 176 verses), in breadth (from personal to universal) and in depth (from joy to sorrow). They were written to be read aloud and heard, not dissected. Many are ascribed to David, the sons of Korah, the sons of Asaph, and one (Psalm 90) even to Moses.

Where there is a heading, we can gain some clues to the plot behind the passion. There are different types of psalm. The majority are called laments, a form used when facing trouble. They reflect fairly honestly what often motivates us to pray!

Properly used, the psalms can help us to grow in our relationship with God, mature in our life of faith, and, become more fully human. Their poetry slows us down and takes us deeper into ourselves. Their spirit of prayer ensures that we do not remain there, but turn to God and deal directly with him. The best way to get into the psalms is to read them yourself. They call us to raw spirituality and authentic intimacy with God.

20. Proverbs – practical wisdom – conduct

The third book of wisdom is Proverbs. There is always a danger of becoming detached from life when taken up with God. We should rather

> [Proverbs] is about living the life of faith in the world.

become more involved and more human. Proverbs is concerned with ordinary experience: how to live well. It has to do with work and money, sex and marriage, home and family, friends and conversation, food and drink, emotions and attitudes. There are 900 proverbs covering all of life, with multiple contributors: this book was written over centuries. It is a relevant book rather than a religious book. It is about living the life of faith in the world. The key to a good life is *moral* not *material*, and so it establishes patterns of good behaviour.

Chapters 1–9 Instruction on wisdom – fifteen sonnets

Chapters 10–24 First collection of proverbs

– 375 maxims on practical morality
10–22: mostly statements, gathered by Solomon
22–24: some sayings come out of Egypt and Babylon

Chapters 25–29 Second collection of proverbs

– maxims on practical morality
– mostly word pictures, gathered by the men of Hezekiah 200 years later

Chapters 30–31 Appendix

30: sayings of Agur (an Arabic name)
31: sayings of King Lemuel (an Easterner)
– fear God in your hearts, learn his ways, follow him
– acrostic poem on the perfect wife

Wisdom leads to good choices and right living. Folly leads you astray and into sin. A proverb states a general truth that is usually but not always true. A promise states a truth that is always true. Some wisdom here is straightforward – learn from your home, choose your friends carefully, take care when you go out into the world, watch that you are not led astray. The problem with common sense is that it is not all that common!

Here is a feast of truths to dip into and reflect on. Some of the images have become embedded in our culture – the sluggard, the nagging wife, the pestering neighbour, the over-cheery friend. The writer finishes with a poem summing up many of the good qualities of the perfect wife rather than painting a picture of one person. There is no matching one for husbands!

To the writer, many of the best things we learn come from our homes, beginning with faith itself. These are refined by argument and experience, and tested by life. Finally, they are made memorable in short, terse sayings. They are not in any order, reflecting the way advice is given by parents to children. When children leave home, parents are not short of advice. It just spills out, unasked for and sometimes unheard. But in the end it says: go and face life and live it out to the full.

Much of this material comes from the time of King Solomon. His reign had the feel of the Renaissance, with its novelty and excitement. Solomon's ships traded as far away as Africa and India. With prosperity came leisure and a growth in the arts, and the employment, where appropriate, of gifted foreigners in forestry, craftsmanship or seamanship. Everywhere there was a whirl of new activity.

At the same time Solomon's intellectual fame spread and drew the world to his door, most notably when the Queen of Sheba tested his erudition and wit. In these mind-sharpening encounters, beliefs were refined. Wisdom for life was universal. Shared ground existed between the truly wise of any nation.

People flocked to hear Solomon because his wisdom surpassed their own. There was, of course, a store of native wit before Solomon, in the riddles and proverbs of the wise, but it was gathered together and grew significantly in this period. His writings, and those of his companions, succeeded in combining openness with depth, and a searching frankness with a tenacious underlying faith.

21. Ecclesiastes –
the emptiness of materialism –
pessimism

The fourth book of Wisdom, the book of Ecclesiastes, is relevant today when many lack any sense of the reality of God, or a 'big picture' (meta-narrative) by which to shape their lives. If life is only what happens between birth and death, and there is nothing more, can anything make sense of life lived under the sun? In the end, whatever happens and whatever we achieve is so much emptiness.

Ecclesiastes is not an easy book to lay out, as some of its arguments are repeated in different ways. It is helpful to read it right through at a sitting.

Chapter 1 Problem stated

'What is the point of anything?'

Chapters 1–8 Problem studied, evidence gathered

a) Personal experiment (1–2)
b) General observation (3–5)
c) Practical morality (6–8)

Chapters 9–12 Problem solved, effects revealed

a) Review (9–11)
b) Conclusion (12): fear God, trust and obey

Without God to hold it together, life can quickly become baffling and confusing. The universe seems to be going round in circles. History has no clear sense of direction. Whatever you do, there are clear injustices in our world. The wise suffer and the wicked prosper. So questions are asked: 'Who am I?' 'What is life all about?' 'Why am I here?' 'Is life worth living?' Do we try and answer these, or is it better to concentrate on one's own experience of life where self is the centre?

The writer portrays Solomon, gifted with youth, wealth, power and opportunity, trying to find meaning in life. He studied to find truth and found the outcome both stimulating and frustrating as he knew more and more about less and less. The more he knew, the more sorrow he felt. He tried enjoying himself to the full but after a time it went stale. Pleasure can become a tyrant and a false god, whether the route is wine, women or song, whether your pleasure is refined or crude. He sought fulfilment in achievement and worked hard. Yet achieve your goal and the pleasure goes. Even what you achieve does not last. The writer looked around and saw how mixed up life was, how little seemed to work out. Leave God out of life and the key to life is lost.

> Without God to hold it together, life can quickly become baffling and confusing.

No wonder in the end the writer comes back to the truth – fear God, trust and obey. Without God, life is a roundabout going nowhere. With God, life has a rhythm and you form part of the tapestry of time. Not that there are not problems to face and questions that remain, but underlying it all we believe that life has meaning, purpose and direction, and that gives hope.

How remarkable that the Bible has within it a number of books that seem to question the Bible! The Bible is never afraid of asking hard questions, though it does not promise us all the answers. Never be afraid of truth! We need today a thought-out godliness, a faith to live by which has the common sense of Proverbs, the tenacity of Job and the sharp honesty of Ecclesiastes.

'The fear of the Lord is the beginning of wisdom' (Proverbs 9:10). This maxim stops the shrewdness of Proverbs from slipping into mere self-interest, the perplexity of Job from becoming rebellion, and the disillusionment of Ecclesiastes from leading to final despair.

22. Song of Songs (or Solomon) – the fulfilment of love – communion

The final book of Wisdom is the Song of Songs, which many know as the Song of Solomon. The title 'Song of Songs' means 'greatest song', for Hebrew has no superlative form for adjectives, hence 'Song of Songs', 'King of kings', 'holy of holies'.

> The Bible is never afraid of asking hard questions, though it does not promise us all the answers. Never be afraid of truth!

This is a very hard book to get into, although there are enough verses in it to make those who dip into it blush. Strangely, it used to be very popular in the nineteenth-century Romantic era, when texts were taken from it regularly. Here is an outline that I have found helpful.

There are seven songs, not in chronological order:

1. Chapters 1:1 – 2:7: wedding day – humble
2. Chapters 2:8 – 3:5: courtship days recalled – hesitating
3. Chapters 3:6 – 5:1: betrothal remembered – happy
4. Chapters 5:2 – 6:3: troubled dream – half-hearted
5. Chapters 6:4 – 7:10: healing of praise – help
6. Chapters 7:11 – 8:4: need to go back to go forward – home
7. Chapter 8:5 – 8:14: renewed love at Lebanon – harmony

Some say the book has no plot at all; it is simply a series of love poems. It may well be. If there is a story behind these poems, then it is an idyll between two lovers, pure and innocent: a girl and her shepherd–king.

The story of Song of Songs

King Solomon, with his courtly retinue, visits the royal vineyards on Mount Lebanon. He comes, by surprise, on a Shulammite woman, to whom he is attracted.

She flees from him. He is too powerful, out of her reach. Solomon then visits her, disguised as a shepherd, and wins her love. He then comes in all his royal estate, reveals himself as the king and calls her to leave Lebanon and be his queen.

They are in the act of being married when the poem opens. She looks back on the uncertainties she felt during their courtship. Even after marriage she struggles to find reality in her relationship. It is all so different from what she imagined. His loving support alone can help her to see the man behind the role of king.

For reassurance, she asks him to take her back to Lebanon. There, on home ground, they renew their love for each other and secure their future together.

That may or may not be the story, but what is it about? Is it an allegory about spiritual love, between God and Israel in the Old Testament, and Christ and the church, or Christ and the believer, in the New Testament? Or it is about sexual love between a man and a woman? I think it is both, though I believe the primary meaning is to do with sexual love rather than spiritual love.

While it can be seen as an analogy in which a love story between a man and a woman helps us to see spiritual relationships more clearly, it is primarily affirming and celebrating human love. 'When the plain sense of Scripture makes good sense, seek no other sense' (David L. Cooper, 1886–1965).

If Job looks at the mystery of suffering and Ecclesiastes at the mystery of existence, then Song of Songs looks at the mystery of love. It encourages genuine intimacy, takes our bodies seriously and does not apologize for being more sensual than spiritual. Within the committed relationship of marriage, sexual love should be expressed and enjoyed. Before that commitment, passion needs to be put on hold, and patience will reap its rewards thereafter. Within love's security there can be genuine mutual giving and receiving. Here love will grow, as love is shown in loyalty and faith in faithfulness.

> If Job looks at the mystery of suffering and Ecclesiastes at the mystery of existence, then Song of Songs looks at the mystery of love.

The Prophets

We turn now to the third and last section of the Old Testament. We have looked at history and wisdom. Now we turn to the prophets. As with the history section, there are seventeen books. Here God speaks: 'Thus says the Lord.' The prophets were God's servants and spokesmen.

Two offices were hereditary: the priests of the Aaronic line, and the kings of the Davidic line. Two offices were appointed directly by God, the judges and the prophets. They were raised up to lead or speak in periods of decline and apostasy.

Not all the prophets wrote books, and indeed none of the early prophets wrote, including Elijah and Elisha. Two of the prophetic books were not classified as such in the Hebrew Bible: the acrostic poems of Lamentations and the stories and prophecies of Daniel.

We can lay them out this way:

Latter prophets	Five rolls	Later writings
Isaiah	Lamentations	Daniel
Jeremiah	(Lamentations was to be read on the	
Ezekiel	anniversary of the fall of Jerusalem)	
The twelve		

Prophetic books both forth-tell and fore-tell. At times the church has been tempted to focus exclusively on one or the other. Often the prophets had two levels of meaning. There was an immediate application for that particular time. Sometimes there was another, going beyond either in general principles, or in predictions about the first or second coming of Christ. But most prophecy was primarily addressed to the age in which it was spoken. While the prophets did announce the future, it was usually the immediate future of Israel, Judah and the other surrounding nations. It was their future, not ours, they announced, a future that is now in our past!

The prophets all wrote in specific periods. It is helpful to try to match the prophets with their history.

The writing prophets of the Old Testament

Each prophet wrote out of the situation he faced as prompted by God. Although each book is different, there are recurring themes.

Israel, N. Kingdom	Prophets	To Assyria	Prophets	Judah, S. Kingdom
			Joel?	Joash (40)
		——— 800 BC ———		
Jehoash (16)				Amaziah (29)
Jeroboam 11 (41)	Amos (from S) Jonah (N)			Uzziah (52)
	Hosea (to Hoshea)			
Zechariah (six months)				
Shallum (one month)				
Menahem (10)				
Pekahiah (2)				
Pekah (20)			Isaiah (to Manasseh) Micah	Jotham (16)
Hoshea (9)				Ahaz (16)
722 captivity				Hezekiah (29)
by Assyrians		——— 700 BC ———		
				Manasseh (55) Amon (2)
		Nahum (s)	Jeremiah (to captivity)	Josiah (31)
			Zephaniah Habakkuk	Jehoahaz (3m) Jehoiakim (11)
		——— 600 BC ———		
				Jehoiachin (3m) Zedekiah (11)
				586 captivity by Babylonians
	To Edom		Exile	
	Obadiah (s)		Ezekiel Daniel	
			Remnant	Leader
			Haggai	Zerubbabel
			Zechariah	Joshua the priest
		——— 500 BC ———		
				Ezra
			Malachi	Nehemiah

The fivefold message of the prophet

1) The holiness of God
2) The sinfulness of sin
3) The necessity of repentance
4) The certainty of judgement
5) The indestructibility of grace

And underlying all – the abiding love of God.

The message of the prophets started with God. A holy God requires right living. The prophets spelt out the implications. They spoke nationally to expose social evils. Individuals were rebuked in so far as they contributed to the social malaise and the national situation.

With the condemnation of sin comes the first sign of God's mercy. God condemns sin to provoke people to turn and repent. God is patient. He delights in forgiving sin. However, he will not ignore sin where there is no repentance. Sooner or later, judgement will happen. Yet even when prophecy has been full of doom and despair, the prophets also speak passionately of the indestructibility of grace. There is hope for us, a new chance and a new beginning. Underlying all these five truths is the abiding love of God. Because God is love, he hates sin and calls for repentance. Because God is love, he must judge and punish wrong, but will first go the extra mile to call the sinner back to himself.

God loves human beings. Elsewhere in the Old Testament there are only a few scant references to God's delight or pleasure in people. Here the prophets proclaim loud and clear that God loves us. God's cries of pain and anger are the cries of a wounded lover, distressed over our lack of response.

In the prophets God announces punishment with the sadness of a broken heart. It hurts God, as it hurts any parent, to punish a child, but if a world refuses to learn righteousness through grace, he must resort to punishment. Yet after every national tragedy – invasions by Assyria, Babylon, Persia – Israel has nowhere else to fall, than back into the arms of God's creative love. Each time after punishment, God promises to begin again, to restore the remnant, to write laws on their hearts, to send a Messiah-deliverer and to breathe life into desiccated bones. God promises never to give up but always to love. This is the God the prophets proclaimed.

> A holy God requires right living.

Supremely the prophets were concerned with the covenants made between God and his people. They called the people back to honour them in spirit as well as in the letter of the law. They held the people accountable for the Mosaic covenant. Though we often think of prophets as 'predictors' they have no interest in the future that is disconnected with the past. In fact their word was 'You don't have a future if you don't remember the past!'

They spoke strongly about religious reality, personal integrity and social justice. The prophets each have a distinctive style. They always ministered in a crisis. They were God's spokesmen, warning, accusing or giving hope as appropriate. Urgently, they wanted an immediate response, calling for transformation. The prophets piled up vivid images to create effect.

Let's begin by looking at the five major prophets.

Five major (= larger) prophets: The nature of the king (all addressed to Judah)

1. Isaiah: eighth century BC
2. Jeremiah: seventh century BC – both before the fall of Jerusalem
3. Lamentations: 586 BC – the fall of Jerusalem – a dirge for a wake
4. Ezekiel: sixth century BC
5. Daniel: sixth century BC – both after the fall

23. Isaiah –
the Lord is king – holiness and
salvation

The first major prophet is Isaiah. Isaiah has exactly the same number of chapters as the Bible has books, namely sixty-six. Moreover, Isaiah splits into two parts, just like the Bible. As we saw in the introduction there are thirty-nine books in the Old Testament and twenty-seven in the New. In Isaiah, there are thirty-nine chapters in the first section and twenty-seven in the second. The division comes before and after the exile.

Isaiah lived over 100 years before the fall of Jerusalem and so scholars have suggested that chapters 40–66, describing life after the exile, were written by another author, 'Second Isaiah', or even into two authors, 'Second and Third Isaiah'.

The scholars can argue it out. I have no problem with Isaiah's knowing events beyond his lifetime, because Isaiah 53 includes a lot of detailed knowledge about events eight centuries before they happened!

Chapters 1–39 Before the fall of Jerusalem – forthtelling

Chapters 1–35

a) Condemnation of Judah (1–12)
b) Condemnation of the nations (13–27)
c) Condemnation of Judah (28–35)

Chapters 36–39

a) Historical interlude, looking backwards (36–37)
b) Historical interlude, looking forwards (38–39)

Chapters 40–66 After the fall of Jerusalem – foretelling

a) Comfort when idols have gone
    – supremacy of the Lord, purpose of peace (40–45)
b) Comfort when the saviour has come
    – servant of the Lord, Prince of peace (49–57)
c) Comfort when God's people are righteous
    – challenge of the Lord, programme of peace

The book of Isaiah divides into three sections. The first section deals with the menace of the coming Assyrians, who, having invaded and vanquished Israel, are heading for Jerusalem.

In the second section we have a short historical interlude in which King Hezekiah, with Isaiah's support, sees off Sennacherib and the Assyrians. But Isaiah also predicts a time when the next superpower, Babylon, will return to overrun Jerusalem.

The setting for the last section, chapters 40–66, is quite different. The people are in exile, looking forward to returning to the land. This section looks further still to the coming of God's anointed servant.

There is something regal about the book of Isaiah, so I have entitled it 'The Lord is king', but unlike any other book I have given it two key words – judgement and salvation.

> [Isaiah has] two key words – judgement and salvation.

In the first half, Isaiah speaks solemnly of judgement, as Israel stands before the holiness of God and is found wanting. There is a wonderful chapter (6) that tells of Isaiah's call and commission, or perhaps his recommissioning, once the long reign of King Uzziah has come to an end. Just when the people were saying 'The king is dead', Isaiah was given a vision that made him say 'Long live the King'. The King, the Holy One of Israel, as Isaiah calls him, rules over the nations. In Isaiah chapter 6 you feel the holiness of God, the prophet's sinfulness and the need for the people to turn.

In the second half the theme is salvation, and hope comes for the exiles through the suffering servant, of whom Isaiah gives us 'five songs'. As Christians we see in the suffering servant a picture of Jesus. The key chapter is chapter 53, one of the best-loved chapters in the Bible.

The first half of Isaiah is summed up in Revelation chapter 4, focusing on the throne, and the second half is summed up in Revelation chapter 5, centred on the Lamb upon the throne.

Isaiah was a prophet of the court and had royal blood in him. A married man, he wrote in a majestic style. He prophesied during the period from King Uzziah to King Hezekiah (four reigns) and tradition tells us he was martyred by the next king, Manasseh. Some say that Hebrews 11:37, which tells of someone sawn in two (tradition says in a log), refers to Isaiah! What Beethoven is to music and Shakespeare is to literature, Isaiah is to prophecy.

Reading the prophets is difficult. Why? Well, primarily because they were not meant to be read but to be heard! These books are mainly collections of spoken oracles. They are not always presented in their original chronological sequence. They are often given without hints as to where one oracle ends and another begins. We do not always have details of their historical setting. Moreover, most of the oracles were written in poetry! And that is all before we face the problem of 'historical distance', because they were spoken firstly into a different religious, historical and cultural setting. Still, there are riches to be found if we are willing to look.

24. Jeremiah –
the Lord is judge – faithfulness
(to Judah)

Jeremiah has been called the prophet of tears. There are parallels with Jesus weeping over Jerusalem on the first Palm Sunday. Whereas Isaiah's ministry would climax in deliverance, Jeremiah's ended with the nation's destruction. He comes across as a sensitive person with a child's heart. However, he was also strong, and faithful to his calling for forty years during the troubled reigns of the last five monarchs of Judah. His book is a mixture of signs, suffering and sermons.

Chapters 1–39 Before the fall of Jerusalem

a) Call and commission (1)

b) Ministry – general and undated (2–20)

c) Messages – particular and dated (21–39)

Chapters 40–52 After the fall of Jerusalem

a) Messages – particular and dated (40–44)

b) Messages to the nations (45–51)

c) Historical postscript (52)

Read through Jeremiah and see how he faced rejection by his family and various attempts on his life by others. He was put down a well and sank in the mud. Finally, coerced to leave the land he loved, he went down to Egypt with the few people not taken into exile. Tradition has it that he was stoned to death.

> God is not a tribal deity. The creator God cares for justice among all nations and speaks to them. In Jeremiah, we see the Lord judging the nation.

In Jeremiah, we see the Lord judging the nation. The key word here is faithfulness, despite a ministry that seemed one of total failure. He had small congregations and saw little response. From time to time people tried to silence him, without success. God's message went forward. The heart of the book is found when you realize that the prophet who spoke sternly to the people also suffered through them and with them. He experienced the consequence of their sins. The prophet declares that God is not detached from sin. Sin wounds the heart of God, for he is not immune from suffering.

God is not a tribal deity. The creator God cares for justice among all nations and speaks to them. Yet more words are addressed to Judah because privilege brings responsibility. They had been given more light.

25. Lamentations –
the fall of Jerusalem – weeping (acrostic songs to Judah)

Lamentations is the postscript to Jeremiah. It is a tear-drenched elegy for the dreadful events on 9 August 586, when the city finally fell to the Babylonians.

Chapter 1 The solitary city – Jerusalem

Chapter 2 Sources of her sorrows

– the Lord's anger described

Chapter 3 The prophet's identification

– Jeremiah's grief

Chapter 4 Desolation

– the Lord's anger defended

Chapter 5 Appeal out of sorrow

– Jerusalem's prayer

The Septuagint has a preface, probably not original, which says that Lamentations was written by Jeremiah. Scripture does not tell us. It would fit in with the weeping prophet who had seen his ministry come to nothing and who had witnessed his people being killed or taken off into exile.

These five poems are acrostic songs. Each verse starts with a different letter of the alphabet so that verse one would begin with A (or its equivalent in Hebrew), verse two with B, verse three with C, and so on. Chapter 3, a much longer chapter, gives three verses to every letter. So verses 1 to 3 begin with A, verses 4 to 6 with B, and so on. There are sixty-six verses in this chapter because there are twenty-two letters in the Hebrew alphabet.

Lamentations is a carefully worked-out poem, not the impassioned outpourings of a broken heart. Someone sat sombrely, beholding a city's destruction, and spelt out what happened in powerful, moving detail. There is something funereal about it.

> [In Lamentations] we find a previous generation also turning away from the Lord.

Read Lamentations and remember the time when Jesus wept over the same city, longing to gather all the people under his love and care. Here we find a previous generation also turning away from the Lord.

26. Ezekiel – the Lord gives hope – glory

The fourth major prophet is Ezekiel. Ezekiel is the prophet of reconstruction. A priest whom God called to be a prophet, he was abrupt, bold and fiery. His message was clear: 'Return to the Lord; then you can return to Jerusalem.' There are no shortcuts. He preached for twenty years in exile.

Chapters 1–3 Call and commission

Chapters 4–24 Present judgement on Judah

Chapters 25–32 Judgement on the nations

Chapters 33–48 Restoration of Israel

Ezekiel grew up under Jeremiah's ministry, and learned from him. He was taken captive at the age of twenty-five, in the second of Nebuchadnezzar's three purges. In the first purge, Daniel went, and in the third Jerusalem fell completely. Ezekiel went into exile about eleven years before Jerusalem finally fell, but did not start to prophesy for another five years, when he was thirty. Thirty was when a priest started in his intended vocation.

By that time he was far away from Jerusalem, with the Temple beyond reach. He was with a group of able high-class exiles living by the banks of the Kebar River (or canal), which flowed into the Euphrates.

Ezekiel gives a far more positive statement about the future of the people of God beyond the fall of Jerusalem. He stresses that the Lord gives hope. The key word of his prophecy is glory.

He starts with the most remarkable graphic vision of God, characteristic of his whole ministry. He often speaks in visions and never loses sight of the glory of God.

Ezekiel prophesied for about twenty years, and for the first six he emphasized Jeremiah's themes. He said to the exiles, 'You seem to think that Jerusalem is indestructible. I tell you, Jerusalem will fall.' Until God is central to your personal, social and national life there is no possible blessing.

Then in chapters 25 to 32 he pronounces judgement on the surrounding nations. These chapters were written while the siege was taking place. The exiles realize now that there is no going back. They are strangers in a strange land. They must learn to speak of Babylon as home. Seeing himself as a watchman set over the people, Ezekiel gives them a new commission. Israel, as a nation, will be revived by God, as a valley of dry bones has life put back into them. Then from chapter 40 he pictures a new Temple. When God is put at the heart of your life, there will be blessing again. Or, as he says in the very last verse of Ezekiel, 48:35, 'The name of the city from that time on will be: the Lord is there'.

> [Ezekiel] stresses that the Lord gives hope. The key word of his prophecy is glory.

27. Daniel – the Lord in charge – providence

The last of the major prophets is Daniel. Daniel served the Lord for seventy years, from the age of seventeen until he was about ninety.

Chapters 1–6 historic

a) Daniel under Nebuchadnezzar (1–4)
b) Daniel under Belshazzar (5)
c) Daniel under Darius (6)

Chapters 7–12 prophetic

a) In the time of Belshazzar (7–8)
b) In the time of Darius (9)
c) In the time of Cyrus (10–12)

Daniel went into exile when he was a teenager, and entered the lions' den nearer the age of ninety! He saw kings and empires come and go. Serving under Nebuchadnezzar in the Babylonian empire, he remained in high office in the Medo-Persian empire and finally in the Persian empire.

No circumstance takes God by surprise. God uses kings and nations to further his perfect will. The key word here is providence.

> No circumstance takes God by surprise. God uses kings and nations to further his perfect will. The key word here is providence.

The book of Daniel divides neatly into two parts, the first half containing the stories that many know. Shadrach, Meshach and Abednego face the fiery furnace bravely. There is the writing on the wall during Belshazzar's Feast, and then Daniel and the lions' den when Darius ruled. The lions, I like to think, were put off Daniel because he was mostly backbone and the rest grit! Perhaps because he did not eat the king's food as a teenager, the lions did not eat him when he was ninety. The first six chapters read more like history than prophecy.

The second half is much harder to get into. One of the most moving parts is Daniel's great prayer in chapter 9 on behalf of the nation. Interestingly, chapters 2–7 are written in Aramaic, while the rest is in Hebrew. Before Daniel's time many people did not understand Aramaic. After him many did not understand Hebrew. During his time people understood both.

The central affirmation is that the Most High God rules. Daniel's book and his prophecies demonstrate this clearly.

The minor prophets

We now move on to the twelve minor prophets, some of whom wrote at the same time as the major prophets. We are unsure of when exactly Joel and Obadiah wrote, but if the rest are broadly in chronological order then these other two may be as well. The first six are addressed alternately to the north and the south; the final six to either Judah or the single kingdom after the exile.

Twelve minor (= smaller) prophets – The conditions of the kingdom

N	Hosea	Eighth
S	Joel	?
N	Amos	Eighth
S	Obadiah	?
N	Jonah	Eighth
S	Micah	Eighth
—		
S	Nahum	Seventh
S	Habakkuk	Seventh
S	Zephaniah	Seventh
—		
S	Haggai	Sixth
S	Zechariah	Sixth
—		
S	Malachi	Fifth

Wherever Joel and Obadiah should be placed, Hosea is out of place. Chronologically it comes after Amos. Hosea may have been put first as it is the longest book (fourteen chapters. Psalms starts the third section of the Hebrew arrangement for a similar reason). Another intriguing possibility is that Hosea's central message should colour the way we read the other eleven, for Hosea speaks of the seeking love of God. The chief sin a person can commit is not the one that attracts publicity, but rejecting God's love. It may be true that people have to fear God's justice before they can experience God's love. In spiritual importance, however, God's love is the key that helps us to understand his justice.

> God's love is the key that helps us to understand his justice.

There are twelve minor prophets. Nine deal with events before the exile, and three (the final three) with events after the exile and the return.

28. Hosea –
decline and fall of Israel –
spiritual adultery

Chapters 1–3 The training of the prophet

– personal affliction
– the faithless wife and the faithful prophet

Chapters 4–14 The teaching of the prophet

– national reflection
– the faithless nation and the faithful Lord

a) God is holy – sin intolerable (4–7)
b) God is just – sin punished (8–10)
c) God is love – Israel restored (11–14)

Hosea mirrors Jeremiah. Both had long ministries and witnessed the decline and fall of their nation. They suffered personally and emotionally as a result of others' sin and enjoyed little visible success. Each has the appearance in parts of prophetic autobiographies. They were prophets of outraged but persevering love.

The secret of Hosea is that he saw to the heart of his subject because he experienced it. His own story in chapters 1–3 is readable and full of pain. Hosea married Gomer. She was unfaithful and slept with other men, although her husband was devoted to her.

When Hosea was feeling most rejected, bitter and down, God said, 'Go back to Gomer, swallow your pride and take her home.' So Hosea did. The words 'So I bought her' (3:2) are filled with humiliation, pain and the priceless nobility of love. What Hosea experienced, God did also.

The Lord explained that, as Gomer has spurned Hosea's love, so Israel had treated him. He had been a faithful husband, yet Israel went off fluttering her eyelashes at other gods. Israel committed not physical but spiritual adultery. She gave her heart to other gods. As your heart has been wounded, so has mine.

The result is a message of impassioned tenderness. It is the people you love best who can hurt you most, from the slight rebuff, the upsetting clash, the stinging hurt of being jilted, the ache of estrangement, to the betrayal of adultery.

God is not detached from our world, watching our misdeeds from afar. He made us in his own image so we could know him and enjoy him. Our resistance grieves him. Israel had sinned against the light, even though they knew God's faithfulness, mercy and goodness to them. Jesus said, 'This is the verdict: Light has come into the world, but people loved darkness instead of light because their deeds were evil.'

In chapters 4 to 14 the story of chapters 1 to 3 is applied to the nation. It is quite difficult to read, perhaps because we have simply headings or sermon notes covering many years. There are some marvellous sentences but the flow of the passages is more difficult. Gifted as an artist, Hosea paints vivid word pictures of a loving God and his mercy towards his stubborn, rebellious children. 'His grief became his gospel,' as Stephen L. Williams Senior puts it in *Discipline of the Wilderness*. The prophet takes themes and returns to them, developing them each time. His verdict on the nation is that 'His hair is sprinkled with grey, but he does not notice.' (7:9).

> God is not detached from our world, watching our misdeeds from afar. He made us in his own image so we could know him and enjoy him. Our resistance grieves him.

The country is in dire straits. Politically there is anarchy and misrule. The throne has been seized by murder, and the state is ruled by military despots. The leaders have been reckless in their foreign alliances. Some enjoy luxurious living at the expense of the poor, and robbery, oppression, falsehood, adultery and murder are common-place. There is much wrong that needs to be addressed.

God is holy, sin is intolerable, and judgement is certain. Yet God is love. So the hope is that Israel will, one day, be restored. Not until the word becomes flesh will God appear as tender and as vulnerable as he does in Hosea.

29. Joel – the day of the Lord – judgement

Chapters 1–2:11 An alarm – day of the Lord

– invasion by a plague of locusts
– desolation

Chapter 2:12–27 An appeal

– eleventh-hour hope

Chapter 2:28–3:21 An anticipation

– the 'after days'
– deliverance

The second minor prophet is Joel, of whom we know nothing with regard to either his background or his nature. His great theme is the 'day of the

Lord'. Israel and Judah looked forward to the day of the Lord as their day of vindication. Joel, however, and supremely Amos, said that the day of the Lord will not be like that. It will be darkness, not light, a cause of sorrow, not singing.

The day of the Lord cannot be confined to a date on a calendar or in an almanac. He says 'This is the day of the Lord'– today. The nation had been troubled by a locust invasion. Such infestations are truly frightening, and devastating to an agricultural economy. You can try to turn locusts back with water, fire, barricades – anything, but you will not stop them. They move forward relentlessly, irresistibly.

Joel says, now that is judgement. The plague of the locusts was the day of the Lord. It was a warning to you. Some people say that the day of the Lord is described in chapter 2, verses 1–11. Others think that this is again an actual plague, returning to clean up whatever has been left behind. Some argue he is using this picture allegorically to describe an invading army and that, too, will be the day of the Lord. Others see in this an apocalyptic picture of the end. Well, it may be an army, then or later, or another literal plague of locusts. Whatever it was, it was the day of the Lord to them. Finally, Joel looks forward to a final day of the Lord, though not to encourage speculation. We need to see every day and every situation as being the day of the Lord. But if the people return to the Lord now, he promises, God will repay them for the years that the locusts have eaten (2:25). What grace!

We have in 2:28–29 the great prophecy of the poured-out Spirit, which was fulfilled on the day of Pentecost. Peter cites this in Acts chapter 2 when he and his fellows are accused of being drunk. For Pentecost was also the day of the Lord, but it was the day of his salvation, an opportunity not to be missed!

> The day of the Lord cannot be confined to a date on a calendar or in an almanac.

30. Amos – accountability for abused privilege – justice

Chapters 1–2 Eight burdens

– exposing and sentencing sin

Chapters 3–6 Three sermons

– revealing social corruption

Chapters 7–9 Five visions

– showing reaction of God

Chapter 9:11–15   Final promise of restoration

Amos and Hosea were contemporaries. Hosea came from the northern cities, while Amos was a southerner called to minister in the north. He was a shepherd from Tekoa, six miles south of Bethlehem, and a tender of sycamore trees (7:12–17).

Whereas Hosea pleaded, Amos thundered. Between them we hear the twin notes of justice and mercy, of God's anger against sin and his love for the sinner. Amos called for repentance. His was a stern and direct message to a corrupt, decadent and inhumane society. The nation had abused the privilege of being the people of God.

The book opens very powerfully. Amos, a foreigner, arrives in the chief religious centre at Bethel and gathers a crowd. Amos begins by making very pointed criticisms of all their neighbours: 'Do you see that nation over there? Judgement is coming on them, and on that one also, and that one'. He goes right round six nations. Their sins are held up to the light of God. Syria was guilty of war crimes; Philistia and Tyre supported a pitiless slave trade; and the hatred of Edom, Ammon and Moab divided communities and stimulated tribal conflict and ethnic cleansing. They depersonalized and degraded their enemies and, of course, themselves.

Then he mentions his own nation, Judah, and God's judgement on them. The crowd lap up the demolition job he does on these nations. They enjoy this. Suddenly he points the finger, saying they are not exempt either! With their defences down, he reveals their social corruption, detailing a whole list of their sins, which demonstrate their avarice and injustice.

This was the last message they expected to hear, for Israel was enjoying a time of peace and prosperity. Prosperity surely meant that God's hand was upon them. Amos made it very clear that they had got their equation quite wrong. 'You are a privileged people. That does not mean prosperity; it means responsibility.'

But though religion was booming, ethics were not. Increasingly a darker side to their religion was emerging, as practices from other religions were added in, blinding them to what they had become.

God is the God of the poor. He saw the poor being exploited by the rich, the rampant greed, the widespread injustice and the materialism fuelled by the women, whom Amos called 'cows'. He did not pull his punches. It was a stern message for a luxurious age. Immorality, corruption, vice and oppression were prevalent. God is concerned not only that we believe the right things (orthodoxy) but also that we *do* the right things (orthopraxis).

Amos gives five visions showing the action of God. Twice, judgement is threatened; the prophet prays, 'Lord, save this people' and God suspends judgement. Then reckoning comes and there is no prayer by the prophet. He realizes what Belshazzar had to realize, that God had assessed the situation and it was too late. God's warnings went unheeded – failed harvests, drought, disease, raids, storms and earthquake.

> 'You are a privileged people. That does not mean prosperity; it means responsibility.'

Yet at the very end we find that judgement is always God's penultimate word. God judges in order to bless. He condemns sin to lead the nation into a peace conditional on righteousness. He, together with Hosea, was God's last-chance prophet. Thirty years after Amos, the nation fell. God will not stand back and do nothing!

31. Obadiah –
principle of poetic justice –
retribution

Verses 1–10 God's judgement of Edom

– doom and destruction

Verses 11–16 Edom's sin against God

– betrayal

Verses 17–21 God's blessing on his people

– deliverance

Obadiah, the shortest of the prophetic books, is one of three prophets called upon to preach doom outside Israel and Judah. Nathan prophesies doom on Assyria, Habakkuk on Babylon, and Obadiah against Edom, a people based just south of the Dead Sea. The Edomites were descendants of Esau, and their opposition to Israel can be traced back to the conflict between Esau and Jacob in Genesis 25.

The nation of Israel took after Jacob, the Edomites after Esau. The Edomites were based at Mount Seir, with their capital the seemingly impregnable fortress of Petra. When destruction fell on Jerusalem in 586 BC, Edom positively gloated at the downfall of their ancient enemy. They marched into the ruins to ransack it. God hates human pride that is arrogant and despises others.

Here is poetic justice. The New Testament states that 'what a person sows, that shall he also reap'. Biblical justice is not simply to deter or to reform but also to punish in proportion to the offence. As Edom betrayed Judah, so they would be betrayed. As they had been cruel, so cruelty would fall on them. They were a godless people, full of pride. They believed that nothing could defeat them – not even God. But they were wrong!

Think of the faith behind Obadiah's vision. A man left with a few poor people, his own country ruined and desolate, and there was Edom sitting in its rock fortress of Petra. Then God says, 'Edom, your time has come. It is Judah that will come back and be a nation again, not you.' History bears that out, for the Edomites were to disappear in the second century. They would be harassed and humiliated from the fall of Jerusalem by successive empires, the Babylonians, the Persians and the Greeks.

> Biblical justice is not simply to deter or to reform but also to punish in proportion to the offence.

In the sixth century Arabs attacked Edom and they had to flee and live as Bedouins. By 450 BC there were no Edomites left in their former lands. By 312 BC Petra was in hands of the Nabateans. The Negev was renamed Idumea after the arrival of the Edomites. The Edomites were forcibly Judaized by John Hyrcanus after the Maccabean revolt. Judaism became their official religion, though they retained their distinctive racial characteristics. In the New Testament it was Herod the Great, an Edomite from Idumea (from a race of great builders), who built Masada, and who tried to exterminate the supreme descendant of Jacob, the Lord Jesus. The rest of the Herod family that followed, including that sly fox Herod Antipas, carried their father's DNA.

Finally they just disappeared, so that there are no longer any Edomites today, anywhere.

32. Jonah – condemnation of exclusiveness – mission

Chapter 1 Jonah and the storm

– fleeing from God

Chapter 2 Jonah and the fish

– praying to God

Chapter 3 Jonah and the city

– speaking for God

Chapter 4 Jonah and the Lord

– learning from God

In Jonah we find not a prophecy but the history of a prophet. It is a much-loved tale, though some Christians are embarrassed by its presence. It seems so far-fetched. The credibility of Jonah, however, does not depend on his edibility. Too often we get hung up on the fish (more a red herring than a whale) and lose sight of a far greater miracle. It may be a miracle that Jonah survived the great fish, but it was a greater miracle that Assyria turned to God. God showed himself to be the God of mercy and mission, an extraordinary revelation.

The book of Jonah condemns exclusiveness. Jonah might have thought of himself as a true patriot, but God reveals him to be a narrow-minded bigot! God chose Israel not as a pet but as a pattern, but they failed to attract others to him. Jonah prophesied in the eighth century BC, when the people were turning away from God and making political alliances with other nations. Yet they were loud in asserting their religious exclusiveness!

> The book of Jonah condemns exclusiveness.

Now Jonah had no desire to go to Nineveh, the capital of the Assyrian empire. Assyria was cruel and vicious, known for its atrocities. Jonah wanted to resign his prophetic commission. His earlier ministry, in the time of Jeroboam II, had been well received (2 Kings 14:25): 'You are going to have great success and your borders will grow.'

But God gave him a new message: 'Go and tell the people of Assyria that judgment is coming to them.' Jonah would not go because, knowing God, he knew that a warning gave time for repentance and forgiveness, which he did not want to see. He did not want a new power on the map to be able to attack Israel, free of the judgement of God.

Well, here is the story in four acts. First we find Jonah and the storm, fleeing from God. Next we find Jonah in the fish, praying to God in words echoing the psalms. Mission resumed, we see Jonah in the city. Nineveh was part of a complex of four cities, Greater Nineveh, sixty miles in circumference, which would take three days to cross. Jonah had a one-line powerful sermon. He gave forty days' notice of the overthrow of the city. The people heard it as a call to repent.

One of the most gracious words in Jonah is chapter 3 verse l: 'Then the word of the Lord came to Jonah a second time.' Some people feel that if they have failed God, the best on offer is God's second best. Not at all! God persists with his people. Jonah was recalled to his great task and was living proof that God does give a second chance to those who will change. Perhaps the unconscious testimony of the bleached-skinned prophet encouraged the city to respond.

The theme of Jonah is mission. God cares for all the nations. Jonah wanted the Assyrians to perish, but God wanted them to repent. Jonah would rather have died than see the Assyrians live, and said so several times! But God was merciful to the penitent Assyrians and God was patient with his rebellious prophet.

Jonah was fed up with God. Waiting to see what happened, he sheltered under a castor-oil plant (very appropriate!). But a worm attacked it during the night and the plant died, which upset Jonah. God used this to explain how much more he cared for Nineveh. The fact that we know the story may be testimony that Jonah learned the lesson.

> The theme of Jonah is mission. God cares for all the nations.

33. Micah – warning under the shadow of the storm – return

Chapters 1–3   Condemnation imminent – judgement declared

a) To the nations (1–2)
b) To the leaders (3)
   – principle of retribution

Chapters 4–5 Consolation – ultimate blessing promised

– promise of restoration

Chapters 6–7 Controversy – present repentance called for (6:1 – 7:7)

– confidence – in the Lord's concern to save (7:8–20)
– plea for repentance

Micah was contemporary with Isaiah. Isaiah was the prophet of the court, Micah of the country places. He came from the hill country overlooking the Philistines' coastal land. From there he could see the great invading armies, moving up and down; Egypt from the south or Assyria from the north.

Micah has been called 'Isaiah in brief'. You can get the central thrust of the first part of Isaiah (1–35) from Micah. He spoke particularly to the people who had been given positions of civic and religious importance.

> 'What does the Lord require of you but to do justice and to love kindness and to walk humbly with your God.'

Micah is more aware of exploitation than Isaiah. He witnessed bribery at every level, and the exploitation of the powerless. Society was becoming more violent, crime was on the increase, and greed led people to cheat. Ruthless landlords took what they could, and evicted those who wouldn't or couldn't pay up. Trading Standards officers would have had a field day looking at the scales and weights used. The result was a breakdown of respect and trust, leading to the disintegration of family relationships.

Micah prophesied that a true ruler from Bethlehem would come and replace all these false rulers (5:2): 'Look south for deliverance to Bethlehem.' Meanwhile, his contemporary, Isaiah, was saying (Isaiah 9:2, 6, and 7): 'Look north to Galilee of the Gentiles for your hope'. It seems an obvious contradiction, until we remember that Jesus was born in Bethlehem but grew up in Galilee.

In Micah we have that wonderful verse in chapter 6 verse 8: 'What does the Lord require of you? To act justly and to love mercy and to walk humbly with your God.' Justice is what we deserve; mercy goes further and gives us what we do not deserve. At the cross, justice and mercy meet in sacrificial love.

The shadow of the Assyrian sword was a warning. It was a call for people to return to God. In Micah's case the people heeded and turned and invasion was put off for many years.

Another lovely verse in Micah is 7:8: 'Do not gloat over me, my enemy. Though I have fallen, I will rise.' It is a great word of hope.

One puzzle to make you think is that Micah 4:1–3 is parallel to Isaiah 2:2–4. So who copied from whom, and why?

34. Nahum –
the end of a cruel nation – sentence

Chapter 1 Verdict of vengeance – declared

Chapter 2 Vision of vengeance – described

– the fall of Nineveh

Chapter 3 Vindication of vengeance – deserved

Jonah went to Nineveh about 770 BC, and Nahum about 620 BC, 150 years later. He was not calling people to repentance, but passing sentence. The clock had run down. What a sad sequel to Jonah. If Jonah said, 'Now is the accepted time', then Nahum said, 'Your time is up!'

Chapter 1 is an acrostic poem. It alternates between a statement to Nineveh of bad news and good news for Israel. It is a marvellous literary work but its message is grim. Chapter 2 tells how judgement will happen, and it is astonishingly detailed. Chapter 3 tells us why God judged Assyria. It was for their sheer inhumanity, not for breaking the Ten Commandments.

The anger of God is nothing like human temper, hot, passionate, blind and foolish. We confuse wrath with petulant anger or selfish ill-temper. If God cannot be angry then he cannot love. He is always master of his anger and uses it for his purposes. He cannot remain indifferent to sin,

> We cannot remain indifferent to sin, oppression and wrong. The Lord is slow to anger but he by no means clears the guilty.

oppression and wrong. The Lord is slow to anger but he by no means clears the guilty.

In the New Testament, being angry is not in itself sin. Paul writes, 'In your anger do not sin: Do not let the sun go down while you are still angry.' (Ephesians 4:26).

The supreme commander Sennacherib taunted Jerusalem and mocked God. These people despised God and were cruel to others. Very solemnly, Nahum foretells their end: Nineveh will fall. That great city of twelve hundred towers, with a circumference of fifty miles, broad enough for three chariots to ride abreast, and with walls a hundred foot high, was finally brought down when the Babylonians diverted the river, undermined the walls and destroyed the people. This all happened in 608 BC.

Today, Nineveh is a desert, a place for wild beasts. Even its location in Iraq is uncertain. Nahum never returned to Israel. His tomb is on the west bank of the Tigris. Capernaum, also in rubble today, is named after Nahum.

35. Habakkuk –
from fear to faith – dialogue (to Judah)

Chapter 1 Faith grapples with problem – sighing

– protests – prophet troubled

Chapter 2 Faith grasps the solution – seeing and silenced

– profound providence – prophet taught

Chapter 3 Faith glories in solution – singing

– powerful praise – prophet triumphant

Habakkuk prophesied twenty years after Zephaniah. King Josiah has been foolishly killed and the nation's decline continues unchecked. Habakkuk is addressing God and the people can overhear what is said.

He starts by saying, 'Lord, I pray and nothing happens. People have no time for you and you do nothing'. Profound questions are raised that echo down the years. If God is good and all-powerful, why do the innocent suffer and the guilty go free? Why doesn't God do something about the mess that the world is in? Habakkuk is not afraid to address God in honest doubt. There are many today who are still troubled by the deafening silence of God.

Habakkuk wrestles boldly and honestly with God until he is given answers. He believes in interrogatory as well as intercessory prayer.

God replies, 'Something is happening in your lifetime. Open your eyes a bit wider. You are in for a very big surprise. I am raising Babylon up to come and destroy you!' Habakkuk is shocked. God's ways are truly not our ways!

And for Habakkuk that raises a far bigger problem: 'We may not be good, but we are better than they are.' The Babylonians were the first nation to implement a scorched-earth policy. Habakkuk fears that nothing will be left! He pleads, as Abraham had for Sodom, 'What of the righteous in the city? It is all too much.' Habakkuk says, 'I'm done with talking. I'm sitting down to watch what happens.'

> If God is good and all-powerful, why do the innocent suffer and the guilty go free? Why doesn't God do something about the mess that the world is in?

God says, 'I know what I am doing. I have seen the evils in Judah that you feel so helpless about. The Babylonians are my instrument of judgement against you but they themselves will also be judged. Whereas they will end in destruction, for you hope remains. My judgement is discriminate, my ways are perfect and I will spare those who live by faith. So get down from your walls!' says the Lord. 'You've got work to do. Write down my words on a wall (biblical graffiti!); get the people ready. The day will come when 'the earth will be filled with the knowledge of God as the waters cover the sea' (2:14).

'The just [NIV, righteous] shall live by faith' (Habakkuk 2:4) is quoted three times in key sections of the New Testament (Romans 1:16–17; Galatians 3:11; Hebrews 10:38). This verse is a cornerstone of the doctrine of justification by faith. In Romans the emphasis is on the word 'just', in Galatians on 'faith' and in Hebrews on 'live'. Here the righteous

> Although he can't see God at work just yet, he believes that God will act when the time is right. He trusts in God's future protection.

(or just) will survive, provided they remain faithful to God. But they must go on believing; they must keep faith (i.e. be faithful). He who endures to the end shall be saved. True faith continues to believe, whatever happens. It does not refer to a single act but to a continuing attitude, 'keeping faith'.

The final chapter of Habakkuk shows his accepting God's will and singing a great song of praise and prayer to God, despite all the hardships that lie ahead. Although he can't see God at work just yet, he believes that God will act when the time is right. He trusts in God's future protection.

36. Zephaniah – through judgement to blessing – vindication

Chapter 1–2:3 Look within – wrath coming on Judah

– declaration of retribution

Chapters 2:4 – 3:8 Look around – wrath on all nations

– exhortation to repentance to five nations
– day of the Lord

Chapter 3:9–20 Look beyond – after wrath, healing

– promise of redemption

Zephaniah is the last of the pre-exilic minor prophets. He was Judah's first prophet for seventy years, since Isaiah. He came from a high-born family and may have been a descendent of King Hezekiah. He is the only

prophet who traces his ancestry back for four generations. He
was contemporary to the other outstanding king of the last days
of Judah, Josiah. Did he help promote revival during Josiah's
reign?

> Zephaniah calls for repentance and then promises healing and hope.

We know nothing about him except that he was a prophetic
contemporary of Habakkuk and Jeremiah. He had a very similar
sort of message, proclaiming God's punishment on the people and on
other nations also. He calls for repentance and then promises healing
and hope.

He also speaks of the day of the Lord, not as a 24-hour period but as
an era of time. This will be the day of God's judgement, when wrongs are
righted, righteousness is vindicated and wickedness is punished; the day
for settling accounts.

37. Haggai –
give God first place – consider

Chapter 1 God's call to work – word of reproach

– to arouse: first day of the sixth month

Chapter 2:1–9 God's call to hope – word of support

– to encourage: twenty-first day of the seventh month

Chapter 2:10–19 God's call to thought – word of blessing

– to confirm: twenty-fourth day of the ninth month

Chapter 2:20–23 God's call to assurance – word of promise

– to cheer: twenty-fourth day of the ninth month

After returning from exile there was a new tone to the prophets' ministry. They were trying to build up a discouraged remnant, not break down a complacent community.

Haggai was the first of the post-exilic prophets. His book covers less than four months and these four prophecies are all we have.

His was a very short but distinct ministry, and its impact was devastatingly effective. The people had come back to their land under the leadership of Zerubbabel and Joshua. They had started to rebuild the Temple, but through political edict and local opposition they had been prevented from completing the work for fourteen years.

Haggai and his contemporary, Zechariah, were called to encourage the people to get back to priorities. They were not to sit around discouraged, but to fulfil their God-given task. Zechariah's ministry lasted for two years and his prophecies are also carefully dated. They overlapped by just one month in 520 BC.

The remnant was meant to be a living witness to God. So Haggai stirred them up to complete the Temple. He spoke in prose not poetry, for he wanted to stir not their feelings but the people themselves into action. Make the main thing the main thing. They had got cause and effect the wrong way round. They said, 'It is not the right time to build the Temple, because we haven't got the energy or money'. Haggai said, 'The crop failure and the rapid inflation came because you stopped building the Temple! When you stop putting first things first, then things go wrong. Compare the standard of your homes and the Temple to see where your priorities lie.' The people responded by starting to build once more.

> When you stop putting first things first, then things go wrong.

The older people discouraged them by making unhelpful comparisons with Solomon's Temple. Better to begin small though, than not start at all. Haggai reminded them of God's promise to be with them. God will fill the Temple with his glory and the Temple will return to its former splendour. Haggai then promised that the royal line would continue through Zerubbabel, and so it did. Every time they flag, Haggai either encourages or challenges them, and in the end the work gets done.

38. Zechariah – Old Testament apocalypse – consummation

Chapters 1–8   Chosen people and the Temple

– Temple being rebuilt
1–4: Five visions of grace
5–6: Two visions of judgement
7–8: Fasting and feasting

Chapters 9–14   Messianic king and the kingdom

– after the Temple is rebuilt

Zechariah is parallel to but junior to Haggai. This book is longer (twelve chapters not two), and more difficult to understand. Zechariah was later than Haggai and continued to prophecy for longer. Haggai dealt with the present and its immediate problems, but Zechariah looks into the far distant future. There is a lot more poetry in Zechariah, especially in chapters 9–14. Zechariah is strongly visual, full of symbols and graphic pictures, including of animals and angels.

Chapters 1–8 seem to endorse Haggai's message with eight different visions. They are still rebuilding the Temple, in response to Haggai. After the exile, the people listened to the prophets. Zechariah reminded them that when their forefathers had not listened they went into exile!

When Zechariah looks into the future in chapters 9–14, it is more confusing. The time and order is not clear. You don't know how the pieces all fit together, for there is no picture on the lid! There is a change of style and content. These chapters do not mention the Temple, Zerubbabel or Joshua. They have a different feel. Zechariah is looking to the future and to the coming king and the kingdom. The only book in the New Testament that is comparable to chapters 9–14 and Daniel 7–12 is the final book, Revelation. Zechariah is very different from Haggai: Haggai speaks in down-to-earth prose whereas Zechariah is an up-to-heaven visionary. Yet both prophets have similar ideals and identical ambitions.

Zechariah forecasts two important developments. Firstly, priests would replace prophets as the spiritual leaders of the community (Zechariah was a priest–prophet himself). Secondly, the priests would take over from the kings as leaders (Zechariah made a crown of silver and gold and put it on Joshua, not Zerubbabel). There are also a number of passages that are taken up in the Gospels. Three of these are Jesus riding into Jerusalem, in 9:9 (Matthew 21:4, 5); being pierced for us on the cross, in 12:10 (John 19:37); and the Shepherd being cruelly smitten, in 13:7 (Matthew 26:31; 1 Peter 2:24, 25).

> Zechariah is looking to the future and to the coming king and the kingdom.

39. Malachi –
press on to the goal – apostasy

Chapter 1:1–5 Fundamental affirmation – God's unfailing love

Chapter 1:6–2 Formal accusation – humanity's unfaithful conduct

a) Religious decline
– priests appealed to by the Lord (1:6 – 2:9)
b) Social debasement
– people appealed to by Malachi (2:10–16)

Chapters 3–4 Final annunciation – God's unchanging character

a) The coming day will judge the guilty (3)
b) The coming day will bless the godly (4)

Finally we come to Malachi, who, as a near contemporary of Nehemiah, seeks to keep the people faithful to their calling. In the life of faith we often need not new truths but rather to know how to apply old truths in contemporary and realistic terms.

There are some distinct features about this book. There is more of God's speech in Malachi than in any other prophet. Eighty-five per cent of the text is made up of the direct words of God. We know nothing about Malachi himself. He is anonymous; his name means 'messenger'. He is the one prophet who has a dialogue with people. When he is heckled, he responds.

This book was written 100 years after the return from exile, but Jerusalem remained relatively deserted and the surrounding farmland largely barren and uncultivated. Recent harvests had been poor. Swarms of locusts and lack of food made life hard and precarious. The Temple had been finished in 520 BC but was very small, and morale was still low. The walls had been rebuilt, but many people preferred the countryside to a city still scarred by destruction and neglect. In general the people were disappointed, disillusioned and even despairing. They were asking questions such as, 'Was it worth returning at all? Where's this kingdom we were going to build?'

And Malachi answered them, having spoken of God's love. He told the people that they were being unfaithful to God. Exile had cured them of idolatry, but they had settled for a formal religion. Temple worship was a tradition, a ritual without reality, not a priority. Giving was grudging not glad. 'What is the minimum I can give?' The priests were no better than the people. They were not bothered as long as they got paid! So the services were conducted carelessly and casually, as if anything would do for God. They were guilty of the sins of half-heartedness and apathy, not apostasy.

These are often the problems that beset second-generation faith. Such indifference spilled over into their moral life. 'Why bother with God?' became 'Why be good?' They got round Sabbath trading restrictions by using out-of-town supermarkets. Consumerism affected family life: 'Why be faithful to God?' became 'Why be faithful to my wife? Trade her in for a newer model!' So there was considerable divorce and remarriage. As a result, the city was full of widows, orphans and abandoned wives, with no welfare-state provision. A

> In the life of faith we often need not new truths but rather to know how to apply old truths in contemporary and realistic terms.

shortage of eligible women meant the men were marrying outside the people of God and losing their distinct identity.

In reply the people justified themselves: 'God is not bothered about us, so we are not bothered about God!' 'God has stopped loving us, so we've stopped loving him.' 'We can't believe in a God of love – just look at the situation we're in. We have to look after ourselves. He's abandoned us so we might as well look after number one.'

Malachi responds, 'It is mercy, not indifference, that holds God back. God said "Return to me and I will return to you".'

He finishes his prophecy by saying that there is a division. Those who will not turn will be judged by God. Those who trust he will bless.

Malachi mentions Moses (lawgiver) and Elijah (prophet). Moses had called them to obey the law, and Elijah to return to it. Take them seriously. Act before it is too late. Their final chance will be through a prophet like Elijah who will come to prepare the way of the Lord. Listen to him when he comes.

We have come to the end of the Old Testament. It started with a perfect world that was 'very good'. It ends with a curse. For four hundred years no prophetic voice is heard, until John the Baptist begins to preach of the coming of Jesus. Through him God's voice is heard once more.

Between the Testaments

I hope that, after our journey so far, you can see how understanding the Old Testament enlarges our understanding of the New. The events of Bethlehem and Calvary were not totally unexpected, but rather the culmination of God's purposes to bring salvation to the world.

As we have travelled together, I hope that parts have been opened up enough to make you want to go back and study them further.

If we had only the Old Testament there would have been a number of unanswered questions. For instance, the ceremonies, priesthood and sacrificial system hinted at something beyond themselves. At the end of the Old Testament the Temple became a centre of dissension and religion corrupt, and the sacrificial system an excuse to avoid obedience. Was there not more to these ceremonies than that?

We have seen that God chose Israel to witness to the living God, to make known his glory to the surrounding nations. Yet at the end we find this nation reduced to a remnant under the control of various superpowers. So what was their destiny, and why was it not achieved?

We saw in the wisdom literature how they had a real knowledge of God and yet there was always something missing, a longing for something just beyond their reach.

Finally, the prophets spoke to their times but also hinted at a day that was to come, when their words would be even more fulfilled.

If we had just the Old Testament, then many prophecies and promises would remain unfulfilled. On its own the Old Testament is like an unfinished symphony. That is why we need the New, for the New added to the Old provides us with a completed masterpiece. We are impoverished if we seek to detach the Old from the New, or the New from the Old. Since the time of Augustine people have recognized that 'the New is in the Old concealed, the Old is in the New revealed' and affirmed the continuity and development of the two Testaments. If you confine yourself to the New you miss the starting point.

Three of the central Old Testament figures were the prophet, the priest and the king. People wanted a prophet, to reveal God to people, greater than the greatest prophet of them all, Moses. People longed for a priest, who could stand between them in their sin and God in his holiness. They looked for someone greater than Aaron, the first great high priest. People hoped for a king, to rule effectively. Their model was King David.

They looked for one who would be prophet, priest and king, and this the New Testament provides. Jesus Christ came as prophet, not just speaking God's word but as the Word made flesh. He came as our great high priest, standing between God and the people and pleading on our behalf. Yet he was also the Lamb of God, the perfect sacrifice taking away the sins of the world once and for all. Finally, he came as king, David's greater son. He fulfilled the longing for a messiah (or, in Greek, *khristos*, Christ – the anointed). He is the Lord, King of Kings and Lord of Lords.

Now you may be itching to turn to the New Testament, but it is not quite as easy as that. Between the end of the Old Testament and the beginning of the New, many Bibles have a blank sheet of paper. That sheet represents 400 years of history and much happened during that time.

When we left the story, the centre of the empire was firmly in the east. After Assyria came Babylon and then Persia, all based in Asia. When we turn to Matthew's Gospel, the centre of the empire is in Europe and its capital is Rome. Persia has been replaced by Rome as the dominant power. Artaxerxes no longer rules over Palestine; Caesar has appointed Herod the Great to the throne. Even the Temple, the heart of Israel's faith and worship, has changed. The makeshift reconstruction put up by Zerubbabel was being rebuilt in marble and gold and huge slabs of cream stone by Herod the Great. The construction of this Temple had begun in 19 BC. It would not be completed until 64 AD, only to be destroyed six years later when Rome sacked Jerusalem.

> ❯ ... the New [Testament] added to the Old provides us with a completed masterpiece.

Search the Old Testament and you will find no mention of synagogues, yet they litter the pages of the New Testament, not only in Palestine but throughout the empire. Everywhere we will meet them. Greek is now the lingua franca. Many Jews outside Palestine use the Septuagint (Greek) translation of the Old Testament. It is known simply by the figures LXX, supposedly because seventy people were engaged in its translation.

At the end of the Old Testament the only Jewish writings were those contained in the Old Testament itself, but now there are other books. These books (known as the Apocrypha), written between Malachi and Matthew, influenced the culture. They can be of value and interest for Christians, though they are not recognized by most churches as being part of God's word. Finally, those arch rivals of Jesus in the gospels, the Pharisees and Sadducees, did not exist in Old Testament times. They arose in the second century BC.

There are, then, things that we need to have explained if we are going to make the most of our travels through the New Testament. So let me try to fill in the gaps.

After being in exile the Jews became the most monotheistic people in the world. This is 'the dark period', because, for 400 years, prophecy stops. No longer is there a living word of God. The people cannot learn God's will from a prophet. So they turn again to their Old Testament, especially to Genesis to Deuteronomy. That is why the Jews are often called 'the people of the book' (as later the Christians and the Muslims will be). In order for the Law to be understood, a new class of people emerged, called scribes, who were dedicated to expounding and applying God's Law and the traditions associated with it.

Disobedience to the Law led to exile, so extreme care had to be taken not to rebel again. If the people were to take the Law seriously, it had to be applied in a different context. This was more complicated because they were rarely ever independent again. How should they relate to those ruling over them while still being faithful to God? Was it to be compromise or resistance? To make doubly sure of doing the right thing they included a safety margin in their interpretations to hedge them into obedience.

The problem was that the hedge became more important than the Law itself. They multiplied regulations until they became a wearisome burden on people.

The scribes modelled themselves on Ezra, priest and scribe. After he preached from the Law, he sent leaders among the people to explain its sense. Two of the most famous scribes, Shammai and Hillel, were living when Jesus was born. In Matthew 19 the Jews ask Jesus about divorce because these two great leaders disagreed on this. Whom ought they to follow? Jesus said neither, and went back to God's Law, not human interpretation. Look at God's original plan for marriage and see God's good intention. Desire for reconciliation should come before grounds for divorce.

With the scribes came the leadership of the priest. They carried not only religious but, increasingly, also civil authority. They were seen as the people to deal with. When civil power is given with religious authority, people aspire to position from mixed motives, and intrigue and conspiracy develop.

Synagogues developed as an alternative provision for worship, when the Jews were far away from the Temple. As time passed, the Temple's hold on people's loyalties loosened. Many had never known Temple worship at all. So wherever there were ten male Jews, a synagogue could be constituted. People would gather to hear the Law being read and expounded.

From the synagogue we get the beginning of preaching and our model of the church. Elders and deacons, roles found in our New Testament, are all part of the synagogue. The synagogue was used as a law court, a community centre and a school during the week.

As the scribes interpreted and applied the Law, so they added to it, until, for many, the oral law became more important than the written Law. These oral traditions became a blight because they hardened and blinded the people to the living truth of Christ.

After the Persians came the Greek empire, from 331 to 63 BC. Alexander the Great conquered the world in ten years. He defeated the Persians and conquered Asia Minor, Tyre, Gaza and Egypt, going as far east as Afghanistan and India. At the age of thirty-three he died, a broken man. 370 years, later on the very roads he had travelled, the apostle Paul would take a message about another man who died at thirty-three. But he brought a story not of death and disappointment, but of new life. For the man he spoke of rose again.

Alexander the Great conquered the world and the hearts of the Jewish people. When he came down to Jerusalem he made peace with the high priest. The high priest showed him part of the book of Daniel (chapter 8), prophesying that he would rise and destroy the Persians. He was inspired to do just that. So he was favourably disposed towards the Jews and the Jews responded to him.

Some Jews wanted to be more like the Greeks. They set up the Hellenistic party (more like the Greeks). They wanted to tone down some of the extreme attitudes of Jewish religion and import Greek values and culture. They welcomed its literature and philosophy, Greek games and attitudes. This was especially true of the Jews who still lived in Babylon, in Asia Minor, or down at Alexandria. But not everyone saw things this way. From the start of the Greek period there grew up a tension between those who wanted to follow the new ways and those who resisted them as a threat to their religion and to their lives.

When Alexander died, the empire divided into four. Two parts of it matter to us because they formed the two kingdoms lying north and south of Judea. They would cause constant tension even as the old empires of Egypt to the south and Assyria and Babylon to the north had in the past. The southern dynasty was the house of Ptolemy and that to the north the house of Seleucid. Sometimes the two kingdoms were allies; at other times there was open hostility. When hostility broke out, Judea was caught between the anvil and the hammer.

From 323–204 the dominating power was the southern house of Ptolemy. During this period the library in Alexandria was built and the Greek translation of the Old Testament was made, for Jews who did not understand Hebrew and for those non-Jews attracted to faith in only one God and to the high Jewish moral standards.

From 204–165 the northern house of Seleucid dominated Judea. During this period Palestine was divided into Judea, Samaria, Galilee, Perea and Trachonitis – familiar names from our New Testament.

The most significant event was the rule of Antiochus Epiphanes from 175 to 164 BC. He was believed to be the one referred to in Daniel chapter 9 as 'the abomination of desolation'. Jesus refers to this, when talking about the end times, because of the evil this person did. He opposed Jewish distinctiveness, and wanted Greek influence to permeate society. He sacked Jerusalem and put people to death. He suspended Temple sacrifices, and ordered the scriptures to be burned (not the last time in history that has happened). He forbade male circumcision, Sabbath observance and Jewish food laws. Worst of all, in the Temple he put up a new altar to Zeus, lord of heaven, on which he sacrificed a pig (to Jews the most unclean animal). Some people went along with Antiochus, thinking the Jewish faith narrow and restrictive. But the majority did not. They resisted and faced torture and death as a consequence.

Violent reaction came in the form of the Maccabean revolt. You can read about this in the two books of Maccabees in the Apocrypha. It was an armed uprising against Antiochus for his opposition to the Jewish faith. Two envoys of Antiochus came to an old priest named Mattathias, and he, preferring death to defilement, rose and slew them. Although he himself died shortly afterwards, his sons carried the cause forward by retreating into the hills and engaging in guerilla tactics. They destroyed pagan altars, forcibly circumcized Jewish children, and slew those who compromised. They took on sizeable armed forces with increasing success. Eventually they won their struggle under Judas (166–161), the first of Mattathias' sons to be leader, who had been given the name of Maccabeus, 'the hammer or the eradicator'.

In 164 BC they took Jerusalem. They got rid of the defiled altar and replaced it with a new altar and a new sacrifice. The date of dedication happened to be 25 December. The anniversary was called the festival of the Dedication and it is mentioned in John 10:22, when Jesus goes down to Jerusalem for this feast. He was remembering the day when Judas Maccabeus restored the worship of God in the heart of the city. Imagine how people would be thinking, and then listen to Jesus' words.

The Maccabean revolt was a religious struggle although, as power was involved, it became political. Judas was succeeded by his brother Jonathan (161–143) and then by another brother, Simon (143–135), and by Simon's son, John Hyrcanus (135–106). It was John Hyrcanus who eventually secured political independence in 128 BC. He enlarged the border of Judea and established the Hasmonean line. Also known as the Maccabean line, they ruled Judea for this period. They were priest–leaders.

However, the tension that had started with Alexander was growing, between those advocating Greek ways and those resisting them. The priests, recognizing that their power depended on Greek support, backed the status quo. Behind them came the leading families, the rich, landowning class. They dominated Jerusalem, the Sanhedrin and the Temple. From this faction came the Sadducees. Theologically conservative, they focused on the Torah and were sceptical about some of the Pharisees' cherished beliefs about the resurrection.

Others wanted religious separation. These were the Hasidim, the separated ones. From this faction came the Pharisees, six thousand strong at the time of Jesus. The Pharisees attracted many of the scribes to their party, as the Sadducees attracted many of the priests. The Pharisees had high ethical standards and strong individual piety, believed in resurrection and were guided by the oral law. However, they also could be legalistic, loveless and arrogant.

In general, the Pharisees tried to influence the nation from the people upwards, whereas the Sadducees tried to influence the nation from the ruling power downwards.

Another party that emerged was the Essenes, who saw priests as coveting power and corrupting it. So they rejected the priesthood, the Temple and all establishment religion. They opted out and formed a monastic order, based on highly ascetic and disciplined communities. They looked forward to the day when God would break into world affairs and sort everyone else out and vindicate them. They presented in powerful imagery a strong dualism between good and evil, light and darkness, God and Satan. Essenes do not appear directly in the New Testament, though the Dead Sea Scrolls found in 1948 in an Essene cave confirmed the canon and text of our Old Testament. Some have wondered whether John the Baptist was connected with or influenced by them, but there is no evidence to support this.

One last empire completes our background study. The fourth and final empire that affected the Jews was the Roman. In many ways the extent of its influence was the Jews' own fault. After John Hyrcanus, the Hasmonean party and the Hasidim party began to squabble so much that the whole stability of this region was threatened. So in 63 BC Pompey invaded Jerusalem. He alienated all Jews by going into the holy of holies. From that time on, Judea became a Roman protectorate

In reaction, another group emerged: the Zealots, the freedom fighters. They looked back to the time of the Maccabees when armed struggle led to independence. In AD 6, when Jesus would have been about ten, Judas the Galilean and Zadok the Pharisee led a revolt that ended in bloody tragedy and mass crucifixion. However, the freedom struggle carried on with Judas' sons, Simon and Jacob, and its base was Galilee. Do you wonder, then, that when another man from Galilee attracted crowds there were many who feared political unrest? You can see what lies behind John chapter 6, when some wanted to make Jesus king by force. One of Jesus' disciples, Simon, was a Zealot. A Zealot revolt would lead to the final overthrow of Jerusalem in AD 70 and the destruction of the Temple.

The Jews got a king again for the first time since 586 BC. He had married into the Maccabean line, though his throne was created through friendship with Rome. Herod became king in 44 BC and ruled for thirty-three years. He was a great builder, building Caesarea, the port where Pontius Pilate had his headquarters. He built a temple for the Samaritans. Supremely, he began the rebuilding of the Jerusalem Temple. The process would continue throughout the whole of Jesus' life. Herod was a cruel man. He murdered his children and his wife, and, true to type, we read in Matthew chapter 2 of the murder of the innocents. He was that kind of man. Indeed, to watch his back he started another party, the Herodians, set up to weaken the Sadducees' power. They were simply power-seekers involved in political intrigue. Of course by Jesus' adulthood Herod was dead, and Herod's three sons had taken over the country. Archelaus had taken over Judea and Samaria, Herod Antipas ruled Galilee, and Philip ruled Trachonitis.

Archelaus was useless, and the Romans replaced him after ten years with their own governor. The fifth governor of Judea was Pontius Pilate, who was responsible for Judea and Samaria. Other areas were governed by Herod Antipas and Philip. These were the people in charge at the time of Jesus.

Under Roman rule the Sanhedrin was the leading Jewish civil and civic authority. It consisted of seventy-one people: the high priest, twenty-four chief priests (representing the twenty-four orders of the priests); twenty-four elders (laity); and twenty-two scribes. The Gospels refer to them as the chief priests, the elders and the scribes. They had a meeting place in the Temple precincts.

Set against all these power groups and enthusiasts were the common people, the people of the land. Largely speaking, they were religious Jews who rejected pharisaical impositions and did their best for themselves and their families.

I hope all this background enlarges your understanding and appreciation of the New Testament.

The Gospels and Acts

There are twenty-seven books in the New Testament. These books are arranged not in a chronological order, because the Gospels were not written first, but in a logical one. They begin by telling us about Jesus Christ, his ministry, life, death and resurrection. Then follow incidents from the history of the early church. The central section is made up of letters to churches and individuals. Finally, we have the Revelation of John.

The books divide into three sections: five history books, twenty-one letters and one apocalyptic vision. The five history books divide into four and one. The four Gospels, Matthew, Mark, Luke and John, are followed by Luke's sequel, Acts. The first thirteen letters are by Paul, nine to churches and four to individuals. The last eight are written by other people. If a letter is 'to' someone it is Pauline (except for Hebrews); if it is the letter 'of' someone, it is by James, Peter, John or Jude.

Both groups of letters start with a great doctrinal statement. Paul's collection begins with Romans, which expounds salvation in all its fullness. The other letters begin with Hebrews, which demonstrates the superiority of Christ

Key events in the New Testament

1. Jesus
2. Cross and resurrection
3. Ascension and Pentecost
4. Church
5. Return

We begin with the Gospels. These are the foundation literature of Christianity. Some try to 'harmonize' the Gospels, producing one consistent account from the four. The New Testament gives us four Gospels to

New Testament (order logical not chronological)					
History – Christ		**Letters – church**			**Apocalyptic – consummation**
5		21			1
Gospels	**Mission**	**Pauline (to)**		**Non-Pauline (of)**	
4	1	13		8	1
		To churches	**To individuals**	**General**	
		9	4	1	7	
Matthew	Acts	Romans	1 Timothy	Hebrews	James	Revelation
Mark		1 Corinthians	2 Timothy		1 Peter	
Luke		2 Corinthians	Titus		2 Peter	
John		Galatians	Philemon		1 John	
		Ephesians			2 John	
		Philippians			3 John	
		Colossians			Jude	
		1 Thessalonians				
		2 Thessalonians				

show Jesus from different angles. The Gospels were written by different people to different churches for different reasons. So how they select and arrange their material, and what they include and leave out, is all intentional. We can benefit from their editorial control.

> [The Gospels] are the foundational literature of Christianity.

The Gospels give four characteristic expressions of Jesus. They are not biographies of Jesus, more pen-pictures, memoirs or impressions. The Gospels are documents of faith, written to help others come to faith also. They are history, telling Jesus' story. They are biography, centred on Jesus. Supremely they are testimony, as Jesus' first followers reflect on him from the right side of the cross and resurrection.

Each Gospel gives so much space to describe the last week of Jesus' life that they have been described as 'passion narratives with extended introductions'. From a quarter to a half of each Gospel is given to the last week of Jesus' life (in Matthew, seven out of twenty-eight chapters; in Mark six out of sixteen; in Luke five out of twenty-four; and in John ten out of twenty-one).

Wherever you look, the person of Jesus stands out. Jesus is revealed as the perfect man, the suffering saviour, the risen Lord and God incarnate. He is the turning point of history, the meeting point of all reality.

The first three Gospels are called the Synoptics (from the Greek for 'see together') because they have a common framework and use the same outline of Jesus' ministry. Scholars try to work out who drew from whom, and what other sources were used. The Gospel form of writing had no precedents before Mark wrote the first Gospel.

John, writing after the other Gospels, takes the shape of the story as known and is able to select, reflect, interpret and comment. Whereas the first three draw largely from Jesus' Galilean ministry, John focuses particularly on his Judean ministry.

A map is helpful to see how Palestine was divided up (see page 140). There were three areas of government: Judea and Samaria; Galilee; Trachonitis, Perea and the Decapolis. Jesus often crossed the Sea of Galilee to allow him to move from one area of jurisdiction to another. This prevented any leader from arresting him before his time had come.

It is worth noticing that the obvious route between Judea and Galilee was through Samaria. Many, however, chose to go down from Jerusalem to Jericho, proceed up the Jordan Valley and then climb up to Galilee. This was to avoid contact with the Samaritans. This adds an extra dimension to the parable of the Good Samaritan, as the man was attacked on the route taken by those who wanted, at all costs, to avoid meeting a Samaritan!

The life of Jesus – key moments

- Birth and boyhood
- Baptism and temptation
- Ministry – signs and sayings
- Confession and transfiguration
- Journey to Jerusalem
- The last week
- Crucifixion, resurrection and ascension.

Here is the basic shape of the life of Jesus. Only two Gospels (Matthew and Luke) start with the events of his birth, but all four recognize the importance of Jesus' baptism by John the Baptist, Jesus' relative. From there he is thrust into the wilderness to be tempted, and returns to begin

Palestine at the time of Christ

his public ministry. He preaches the kingdom of God and demonstrates the power of the kingdom by signs and wonders.

As his ministry progresses, opinion divides and hardens between his followers and his enemies. The hinge in the Gospels comes when Jesus asks the disciples who he is. They recognize that he is more than a great teacher, a healer and even a prophet. Following Peter's confession of this, Jesus concentrates on preparing his followers for the cross. They choose not to hear, however, either resisting or blanking out Jesus' teaching on this subject as it falls outside their own plans and agenda.

The encounter with Moses and Elijah on the Mount of Transfiguration confirms the uniqueness of Jesus to the disciples. From there they head in stages towards Jerusalem and Holy Week. Each day is packed with incident, beginning with Palm Sunday and culminating in Good Friday. Then the twist comes with the wonderful Easter postscript.

The Gospels ring with truth – these things happened. Jesus was not the product of a brilliant imagination. He was human, flesh and blood like us, and yet holy, sinless – not like us at all. As we travel with him through Jerusalem or stand on the shores of Galilee his ministry clearly displays divine authority. By his miracles he delivers men, women and children from sickness, need, oppression, sin and death. He deals with people as he finds them and they are never the same afterwards.

> The Gospels ring with truth – these things happened.

As we draw near to the cross we are reduced to silence as we watch him surrendering himself voluntarily to others. For us he suffered pain, humiliation and death. Then he rose again. No wonder that, living in the light of Easter, the disciples became convinced that Jesus was Lord (Kurios) and Christ (Messiah), the Anointed One.

The Gospels record at least thirty-five specific occasions on which miracles happened. Jesus did not use magic words or incantations. Miracles came about by simple word or touch, and resulted in people worshipping God. They were never done for Christ's personal benefit, but to fulfil the promise that, when salvation came, it would touch both body and soul. His miracles had a teaching aspect to lead people to faith in him, or to increase their faith. They were, as John said, signs for those who would see.

> ... Jesus is no one other and nothing less than God in human form, revealing God to us and reconciling us to God.

The Gospels focus on various aspects of Jesus. To Matthew, he is the king long promised. Mark emphasizes the strong worker come to serve and sacrifice himself. Luke, the gentile, sees how the Greek longing for the ideal, the perfect man, able to share and empathize, finds its embodiment in Jesus. To John, Jesus is no one other and nothing less than God in human form, revealing God to us and reconciling us to God.

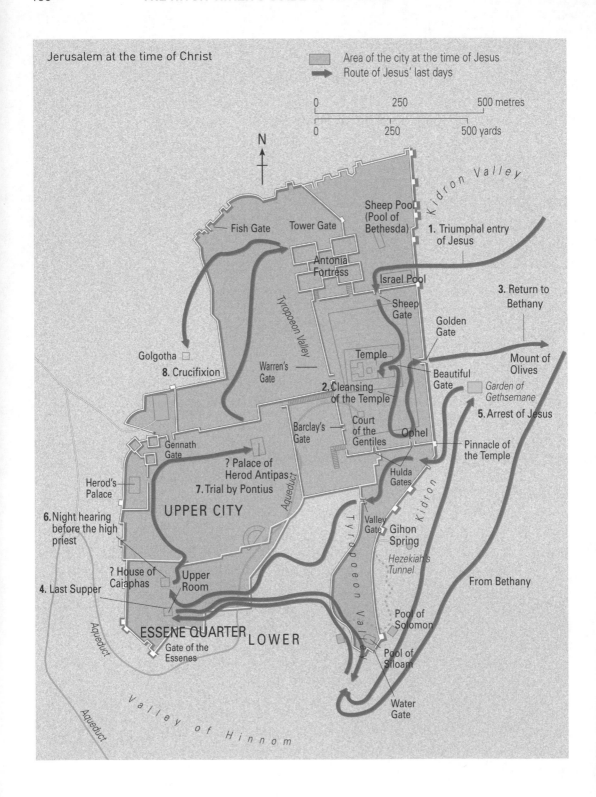

Jerusalem at the time of Christ

Area of the city at the time of Jesus
Route of Jesus' last days

0　250　500 metres
0　250　500 yards

N

Fish Gate
Tower Gate
Sheep Pool (Pool of Bethesda)
1. Triumphal entry of Jesus
Kidron Valley

Antonia Fortress
Israel Pool
Sheep Gate
Golden Gate
3. Return to Bethany

Tyropoeon Valley
Temple
Beautiful Gate
Mount of Olives

Golgotha
8. Crucifixion
Warren's Gate
2. Cleansing of the Temple
Garden of Gethsemane
5. Arrest of Jesus

Barclay's Gate
Court of the Gentiles
Ophel
Pinnacle of the Temple

Gennath Gate
? Palace of Herod Antipas
7. Trial by Pontius
Hulda Gates
Aqueduct

Herod's Palace
UPPER CITY
Valley Gate
Gihon Spring
Kidron

6. Night hearing before the high priest
Hezekiah's Tunnel
From Bethany

? House of Caiaphas
Upper Room
Tyropoeon Valley

4. Last Supper
ESSENE QUARTER　LOWER
Pool of Solomon

Aqueduct
Gate of the Essenes
Pool of Siloam
Water Gate

Aqueduct
Valley of Hinnom

1. Matthew –
the bridge between the Testaments –
fulfilment (16:16)

Matthew, more than any other, makes connections between the Old and the New Testaments. Matthew, the tax gatherer, used his pen to write a different account, an account of Jesus. As befits a book about the king long promised, his style is at times formal and stately. His book may have been used to defend the faith against criticism, as a handbook for those joining the church, and as a lectionary for church worship.

Chapters 1:1 – 4:11 Person of the king

– genealogy – his ancestry (1:1–17)
– nativity – his advent (1:18 – 2:23)
– baptism – his ambassador (3)
– temptation – his advance (4:1–11)

Chapters 4:12 – 16:12 Purpose of the king

– manifesto – Sermon on the Mount (5–7)
– miracles – demonstration of authority (8–9)
  (three times three miracles)
– reaction – belief and opposition (10 – 16:12)

Chapters 16:13 – 28:20 Passion of the king

– disciples prepared (16:13–18)
– journey to the cross (19–27)
– victory accomplished (28)

Matthew divides into three main parts. A king must be of royal descent, so Matthew begins by tracing Jesus' bloodline back to Abraham. His genealogy comes through Abraham, Isaac and Jacob, the House of

Judah, and the line of David. This is the family tree of Joseph, Jesus' foster father, and for legal reasons his bloodline counts. The genealogy contains many well-known names, of both men and women. The women include two foreigners, Rahab and Ruth, and two with chequered histories, Tamar and Uriah's wife, better known as Bathsheba.

The birth stories speak of the wise men's visit to worship the newborn king and the violent reaction of Herod. John's ministry heralds the coming of the king.

In his baptism Jesus identifies with the people in their sins. He then earns his spurs by facing the devil on his own territory. Returning, he proclaims the kingdom and demonstrates its presence. Called the Son of David, he will prove worthy to be king. As his ministry develops he waits until the truth of who he is is revealed to Peter ('You are the Christ, the Son of the living God', Matthew 16:16). Now the nature of his throne can be revealed – a wooden cross. There is a royal sense of occasion as Jesus takes control of all that follows. Others are on trial, not him. Never did any monarch look more majestic than he did as he hung naked and bleeding on the cross. The sky went dark, the ground shook and the dead rose from their graves. When he rose, the whole earth shook, for the King had conquered – what a gospel! Can anyone doubt his credentials? Matthew appeals to Jews to recognize, in Jesus, their long-expected and prayed-for messiah, the Christ.

> Matthew appeals to Jews to recognize, in Jesus, their long-expected and prayed-for messiah, the Christ.

Matthew arranges the teaching of Jesus in five blocks, paralleling the Torah. First the matchless Sermon on the Mount is preached, echoing Mount Sinai and the charter of the people of God. A quarter of Matthew's Gospel is given to the actual words of Jesus.

Teaching in Matthew: Five major teaching blocks

- Manifesto of the kingdom (5–7)
- Proclamation of the kingdom (10)
- Parables of the kingdom (13)
- Fellowship of the kingdom (18)
- Future of the kingdom (24–25).

2. Mark –
the earliest Gospel – action (10:45)

The second Gospel, but probably the first to be written, is Mark. Mark was personal assistant to three great Christians, Barnabas, Paul and Peter. Tradition suggests that this Gospel draws from Peter's preaching. Peter was never afraid of exposing his frailties. Writing for Romans, Mark minimizes Jewish allusions.

The story opens with an adult Jesus and quickly moves from story to story, with teaching and miracles intertwined. There are eighteen miracles and only four parables in this Gospel. This book bustles with life, giving vivid details and picturesque descriptions. There is a breathlessness to this story, as Jesus confronts and masters storms and sickness, demons, disease and death. Here power is shown in service. Facing popularity and hostility, he never loses focus. Service is never demeaning, but power under control. It is power so willing to submit, that, in heroic style, he will lay down his life to complete his mission. 'The Son of Man came not to be served but to serve and give his life a ransom for many' (10:45). He moves decisively from Galilee through Perea, heading for Jerusalem. The pace slows down as he nears Jerusalem and the action halts before the cross.

> 'The Son of Man came not to be served but to serve and give his life a ransom for many.'

Chapter 1:1–1:13 Preparation for service

Chapters 1:14 – 8:26 Servant who serves

Chapter 8:27–30 Peter's confession

Chapters 8:31 – 15:47 Servant who suffers

Chapter 16 Epilogue

Many believe that the eyewitness account of Jesus praying in the Garden of Gethsemane, and the young boy running away, is Mark's own testimony, the Upper Room being in his house. We have not only Peter's confession (8:29) but a second confession from the Roman centurion from the foot of the cross – 'Truly this man was the Son of God!' (15:39).

3. Luke –
the wideness of God's mercy – universal
(19:16)

Luke's Gospel is beautifully written, reflecting careful research. Luke may have conducted his field studies while Paul was in prison in Caesarea. Luke is the first church historian. As a doctor, he would have been uniquely placed to get the 'inside story' of Mary's confinement. He also records Jesus' family tree, but this time through Mary's bloodline. Again it passes through all the right people but continues back to Adam, the first human.

For Luke's Jesus is not just the Jewish messiah, but saviour of the world, of Jews, Samaritans and Gentiles. Here is the dilemma. Because of the seriousness of sin, only God can save us. It is, however, humanity that needs to be saved. So God became a man to be like us enough to save us.

What a feast of parables are found here (thirteen unique to Luke), including the good Samaritan, the prodigal son, and the Pharisee and the tax collector.

Chapter 1:1 – 1:4 Prologue – motive, method

Chapters 1:5 – 2:38 Coming of the Son of Man

Chapters 2:39 – 4:13 Growth to maturity

Chapters 4:14 – 9:50 Ministry in the light of the cross – Galilean

Chapters 9:51 – 19:27 Ministry on the way to the cross – Perean, Judean

Chapters 19:28 – 24:53 Triumph of the Son of Man

– great conflict (19–23)
– grand conquest (24)

Luke is the only Gentile writer, but his two-volume work, the Gospel of Luke and the book of Acts, makes up 27 per cent of the New Testament. His Gospel is full of Christmas songs, known best by their Latin names: Benedictus, Ave Maria, Magnificat, Gloria in Excelsis, Nunc Dimittis. This is the Gospel of forgiveness, prayer, praise and the Holy Spirit. Jesus works his miracles as a person perfectly filled with the Spirit. It is a down-to-earth Gospel with a brushstroke of angels. Jesus is often found eating, drinking and attending parties. No one is excluded – women, children, outcasts, sinners, you and me. As Luke writes (19:16), 'the Son of Man came to seek and to save those who were lost'. Luke's Jesus is the man for others, and he shows the wideness of God's mercy, giving the fullest life story of Jesus we possess.

> This is the Gospel of forgiveness, prayer, praise and the Holy Spirit.

He has his unique slant on the cross and a wonderful chapter on the resurrection that includes the famous journey to Emmaus (among five unique stories in this Gospel). Now that was some hitch-hiker! In chapter 24 we see an open tomb, open scriptures, open eyes, open doors, open understanding, an open heaven and open lips. That is what resurrection does when it is fully understood.

4. John –
that you may believe... and have life
(1:14, 18)

The final Gospel, called the Fourth Gospel or John's Gospel, stands apart.

Chapter 1:1–1:18 Prologue: the incarnation

– God manifest

Chapters 1:19 – 12:50 Public ministry of Jesus to Jews

– in the world

Chapters 13–17 Private ministry of Jesus to 'his own'

– for his followers
– love speaking

Chapters 18, 19 Tragedy

– love suffering
– on the cross

Chapters 20, 21 Triumph – love overcoming

– in new life

John shapes his Gospel round seven sayings of Jesus, each beginning with 'I am' (the bread of life, the light of the world, the gate, the good shepherd, the resurrection and the life, the way, the truth and the life, and the true vine). His account is full of memorable encounters – with Nicodemus, the woman at the well, the nobleman, the lame man by the pool, the woman caught in adultery and the man born blind. There are lengthy discourses, not easy to read, often following a miracle or a memorable saying.

Half of this Gospel is taken up with his passion (literally, 'suffering'). He gives an extended account of the upper room. His account of Jesus washing the disciples' feet, his teaching about the vine and the Holy Spirit and his prayer for his disciples (and for us) make you feel that you are on holy ground.

John confesses that space has limited his selection. His choice was based on 20:31: 'These are written that you might believe that Jesus is the Messiah, the Son of God, and that by believing you might have life in his name.' If Matthew wrote for Jews, Mark for Romans and Luke for Gentiles, then John wrote for the church. He wanted Christians to get a bigger view of Jesus. No family trees, childhood stories or birth accounts are included. However, he goes further back than the others, tracing Christ's coming before creation to the eternal heart of God. The coming of Jesus was pre-planned, an expression of the love of a God who gave his Son that we might live through him. John's beginning echoes Genesis 1 in describing God's new creation in Jesus Christ: 'In the beginning was the Word and the Word was with God, and the Word was God... The Word became flesh and made his dwelling (literally, 'tabernacled') among us. We have seen his glory (literally, *shekhinah*) (John 1:1, 14).

All four Gospels leave us asking, 'Who is Jesus?' All agree that he was fully human, with a human body and human emotions. But clearly he was more than human, and we have to contrast his seemingly ego-centric claims with his selfless and serving spirit. What he said would sound insane if said by anyone else, but his conduct was always so poised and balanced. Here are the paradoxes that emerge. His teaching appears proud, but he was humble. His words were self-centred, yet his actions were self-giving. He called people to himself, forgiving the penitent and rebuking the hard-hearted. He cannot be dismissed as simply a 'good man'. He was either a liar (in which case deceitful and bad) or a lunatic (in which case deluded and mad), or else he was who he claimed to be, Lord of all (in which case he is divine, God made flesh)!

> 'These things are written that you might believe that Jesus is the Christ and that believing you might have life in his name.'

To find out about Jesus, read the Gospels, look at his character, his claims and his conduct, and make your own judgement. Supremely, it is by the events concerning the cross and the evidence of the resurrection that most have been persuaded, many to say, like Thomas, 'My Lord and my God'.

There is an artlessness to the description of the resurrection. No attempt is made to harmonize the accounts or to eliminate discrepancies. The first witnesses were women, despite their testimony not being acceptable in court at that time. But, outdoors and indoors, to individuals, small groups and large gatherings, Jesus appeared. He was the same but different. Not immediately recognizable but, once recognized, clearly Jesus. He could appear and disappear, and pass through locked doors. He would eat meals and allow physical contact. Over six weeks, accounts are given of his risen presence that confirmed his absence from the tomb. His dead body was never exhibited. All the alternative explanations, from not dying to grave-robbers to a carefully spun story, do not stand close examination. Frightened disciples faced death boldly for this truth. The reason was simple. It was impossible that death should hold him. Christ was raised from the dead!

> There is an artlessness to the description of the resurrection. No attempt is made to harmonize the accounts or to eliminate discrepancies.

5. Acts of the Apostles – the beginning of the Church – mission (1:8)

In the gospels we hear Jesus' story; the rest of the New Testament spells out the consequences for ourselves, the church and the world.

The link between the gospels and the letters is Acts. Without this bridging book we would move from a brief account of the ascension to having to deduce all subsequent history from the letters. Acts tells what happened after the resurrection. Without Acts we would encounter Paul in the letters without being introduced to him. Acts tells us his story and describes the emerging church. Without Acts we would jump from a ministry in Palestine to one spread throughout the Roman empire. This book fills in the gap.

Chapters 1–7 Church founded – centre: Jerusalem – key figure: Peter

a) Birth at Pentecost (1–2)
b) Growth through difficulty (3–7)

Chapters 8–12 Church broadened – centre: Antioch

a) In Judea (9)
b) In Samaria (8)
c) To a Gentile proselyte (10–11)

Chapters 13–28 Church expanded – centre: Rome – key figure: Paul

a) To Asia (13–15)
b) To Europe (16–28)

Acts is a thrilling book. Unlike many disappointing cinema sequels, Luke's second volume is as gripping as his first. Traditionally called the 'Acts of the Apostles', the title is deceptive as most of the apostles are not mentioned after the opening chapter. People have tried variations, one of which is 'Acts of Apostolic Men', because as well as Peter and John we have Spirit-filled men such as Stephen, Barnabas, Paul and Timothy. Others prefer 'Acts of the Holy Spirit'. The Holy Spirit is clearly at work, leading the way. The Holy Spirit enabled the birth of the church at Pentecost and provides the dynamic behind the acts of the early Christians. Whatever the virtues of these alternative names, perhaps the more common shortened form, Acts, is the best. After all, acts should always follow the gospel!

Luke's Gospel tell us what Jesus began to do, and Acts what he continued to do, by his Spirit and through the church. Although there is a clear chronology to what Luke presents, he is highly selective in what he includes. To try to piece together a life of Paul from Acts alone would be quite misleading. Significant events in his life are excluded.

This is the story of a vigorous movement. New things are always

> The Holy Spirit enabled the birth of the church at Pentecost and provides the dynamic behind the acts of the early Christians.

happening, and there are new opportunities and new challenges. Opposition grew from outside, and internal subversion was always a danger. Nothing daunted those pioneers as they reached out. Where tradition blocked progress it was reviewed, and, if necessary, abandoned. The great commission had to be obeyed and the work moved forward.

Luke's material shows how the church fulfilled Christ's mandate to be 'witnesses in Jerusalem, and in all Judea and Samaria, and to the ends of the earth' (1:8). This is a book of mission, as the power of the Spirit, the truth of the gospel and consecrated men and women together turned the world upside down, proclaiming King Jesus. Luke focuses on key developments politically, historically and theologically.

The reception of the Holy Spirit (the great compulsion) makes an immediate impact. The infant church grew daily, making an ever-widening impact in Jerusalem (chapters 1–7) and in Judea and Samaria (chapters 8–12). The second half tells how the gospel spread beyond Palestine, planting churches throughout the empire including Rome (chapters 13–28). What progress in thirty years! Once the gospel had taken root in Rome, there would be no stopping it. Individual stories are included if they develop Luke's theme.

Jesus left his disciples to pray, awaiting the promised Holy Spirit. Christ was no longer beside them but, wonderfully, he would be within them. No longer limited by place and time, he could be with all of them wherever they were, whatever they faced.

When the Spirit comes, Peter preaches, handling the word of God in a new way. He presents the gospel clearly and powerfully. It meets with a great response from Peter's first audience, drawn from every part of the empire for the feast of Pentecost. They would gossip the gospel throughout the empire, forming beachheads for its advance in future years.

Peter is central to these opening twelve chapters, as Jesus had promised in Matthew 16, and he is used to open doors to Jews (in chapter 2), to Samaritans (in chapter 8), and to Gentiles (in chapter 10) through Cornelius. The disciples had been utterly transformed. Having let themselves down when Jesus was arrested, they are now filled with holy boldness. Peter who often said the wrong thing now argues eloquently and passionately before those who executed Jesus. Their commitment not to compromise with lies and deception is shown in the terrible story of Ananias and Sapphira (compare Achan's sin). The early Christians give generously to the poor and appoint top-quality leaders to oversee the care of widows and orphans. Preaching is, however, not relegated to second place.

The second major figure in Acts is Saul the Pharisee, better known as the apostle Paul. His conversion on the Damascus road (chapter 9), while heading off to persecute believers, remains one of the great turning points in church history. He became apostle to the Gentiles, committed to going where the gospel had not yet been preached. The tales of his travels, his companions, the sufferings he endured and the churches he planted still remain an inspiration.

It is helpful to read Acts with an open map. During the unfolding story the centre of operations moves north from Jerusalem to Antioch. Then after the eastern end of the Mediterranean has been evangelized, a new base is needed to reach the west. Paul finds himself drawn to Rome, which in the end he reaches.

Paul's three great journeys started in Cyprus (chapters 13–14), where his companion Barnabas came from. Sadly, their companion John Mark turned back. They then tackled their toughest tour in southern Galatia, visiting increasingly remote communities, provoking more and more violent reactions. Despite stoning and expulsion, Paul returned to encourage his infant congregations and to elect leaders to develop the work.

A faction tried to get new Gentile converts circumcized. Paul resisted this and a Council was called in Jerusalem (chapter 15) at which Paul's testimony and Peter's experience was enough to persuade the chair, James, Jesus' brother, that the Council must side with Paul.

In his second journey (chapters 16–18), not being prepared to take John Mark again, he lost Barnabas (Mark's relative), who wanted to give the young man a second chance. Paul took a different route, by land rather than by sea, with a different team. Silas, and then Timothy, joined him and later Luke himself (hence the 'we' passages in Acts). When unsure which way to go, a vision of a man from Macedonia opened the door to Europe (although Europe didn't exist as an entity then). Paul reached its key cities. Some of these he would later write to: Philippi, Thessalonica and Corinth. He visited Athens, with mixed results. He had an extended stay in Corinth and prepared the ground for a lengthier ministry to Ephesus. His strategy was to go to important cities on main

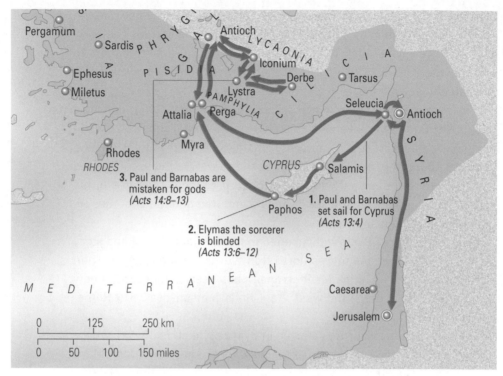

Paul's first missionary journey

Roman roads, plant churches and let the city churches then reach out to the surrounding countryside.

On his third journey (chapters 19–21), he based himself at Ephesus with his good friends Priscilla and Aquila, whom he had first met in Corinth. When he left there he organized an offering for poor Christians in Jerusalem.

Returning to Jerusalem, he was arrested, as had been prophesied, and escaped a lynching only by being transferred to Caesarea (chapters 21–26), where he remained for two years. Despite eloquent defences before Felix, Festus and Agrippa his case was referred to Rome (as he had claimed his rights as a Roman citizen). Following a dramatic shipwreck, he reached Rome (chapters 27–28). There the story closes and tradition has had to fill in the last chapters in Paul's life.

However, we now have the framework to make sense of Paul's letters. As Old Testament history interpreted the prophets and vice versa, so now, in the New, Acts helps us to understand the letters and the letters help us understand Acts. Having been to some of the places and met some of the people in Paul's letters, we feel more at home reading them.

Paul's second missionary journey

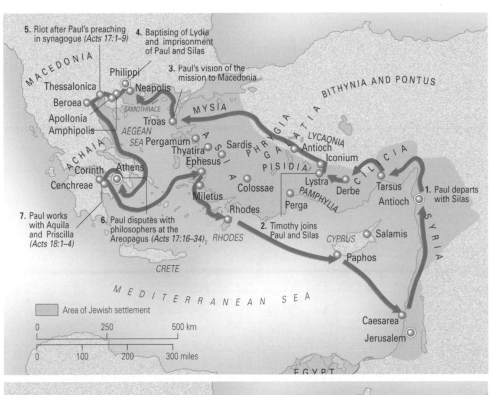

5. Riot after Paul's preaching in synagogue (Acts 17:1–9)

4. Baptising of Lydia and imprisonment of Paul and Silas

3. Paul's vision of the mission to Macedonia

MACEDONIA

BITHYNIA AND PONTUS

Philippi
Thessalonica
Neapolis
Beroea
SAMOTHRACE
MYSIA
Apollonia
Amphipolis
Troas
AEGEAN
SEA
Pergamum
Thyatira
Sardis
PHRYGIA
GALATIA
LYCAONIA
Antioch
Iconium
CILICIA
ACHAIA
Athens
Ephesus
PISIDIA
Corinth
Lystra
Derbe
Tarsus
Cenchreae
Miletus
Colossae
PAMPHYLIA
Antioch
1. Paul departs with Silas

7. Paul works with Aquila and Priscilla (Acts 18:1–4)

6. Paul disputes with philosophers at the Areopagus (Acts 17:16–34)

Rhodes
Perga
RHODES
CYPRUS
Salamis
SYRIA

2. Timothy joins Paul and Silas

Paphos

CRETE

MEDITERRANEAN SEA

Area of Jewish settlement

0   250   500 km
0   100   200   300 miles

Caesarea
Jerusalem

EGYPT

Paul's third missionary journey

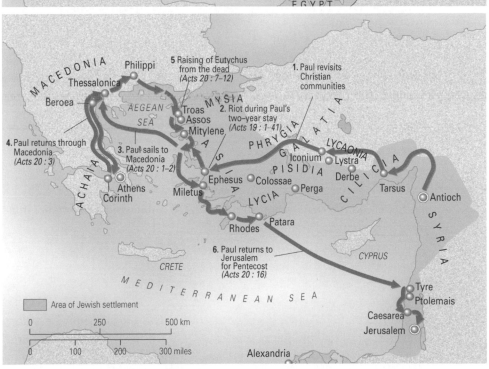

5 Raising of Eutychus from the dead (Acts 20:7–12)

1. Paul revisits Christian communities

MACEDONIA

Philippi
Thessalonica
Beroea
AEGEAN
SEA
MYSIA
Troas
Assos
Mitylene
2. Riot during Paul's two–year stay (Acts 19:1–41)

4. Paul returns through Macedonia (Acts 20:3)

3. Paul sails to Macedonia (Acts 20:1–2)

PHRYGIA
GALATIA
LYCAONIA
Iconium
Lystra
CILICIA
Derbe
Tarsus
Antioch

ACHAIA
Athens
Corinth
Miletus
Ephesus
Colossae
PISIDIA
Perga
LYCIA
Rhodes
Patara

6. Paul returns to Jerusalem for Pentecost (Acts 20:16)

CRETE

CYPRUS
SYRIA

MEDITERRANEAN SEA

Area of Jewish settlement

0   250   500 km
0   100   200   300 miles

Tyre
Ptolemais
Caesarea
Jerusalem

Alexandria

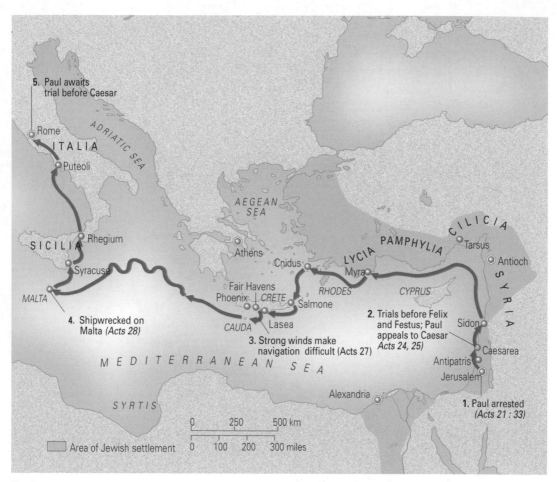

5. Paul awaits trial before Caesar

Rome

ITALIA

Puteoli

ADRIATIC SEA

Rhegium

SICILIA

Syracuse

MALTA

4. Shipwrecked on Malta *(Acts 28)*

3. Strong winds make navigation difficult (Acts 27)

AEGEAN SEA

Athens

Cnidus

Fair Havens

Phoenix | *CRETE*

Salmone

CAUDA   Lasea

RHODES

Myra

LYCIA   **PAMPHYLIA**

CYPRUS

CILICIA

Tarsus

Antioch

S Y R I A

2. Trials before Felix and Festus; Paul appeals to Caesar *Acts 24, 25)*

Sidon

Caesarea

Antipatris

Jerusalem

1. Paul arrested *(Acts 21 : 33)*

M E D I T E R R A N E A N   S E A

S Y R T I S

Alexandria

Area of Jewish settlement

0   250   500 km

0   100   200   300 miles

Paul's voyage to Rome

The Letters

The next twenty-one books are letters. In them we find warmth, energy and passion. They keep our interest. Little personal touches and autobiographical moments give them an immediacy that time and distance cannot dull. They were delivered by hand, carried on the great Roman roads that criss-crossed the empire.

This was a unique window of history when good roads and the Pax Romana (the Roman Peace – brought by the power of the sword!) ensured that the roads were free of bandits and the seas of pirates. It was very different 100 years before, and would be again 100 years later. It was 'when the time had fully come' that the gospel was taken around the world. With Greek widely understood, there were far fewer language barriers except in remoter communities such as Lystra, where language barriers led to misunderstanding.

Letters were more sensible than ours, in that they gave the sender's name at the beginning (emails follow a New Testament pattern!). The address followed and then a greeting, before the substance of the letter was communicated.

When you read other people's letters you hear only one side of a conversation. The advantage of letters is that they are direct and personal. The disadvantage is that you have to try to reconstruct what is happening.

21 Letters

Paul		Others
13		8

Church	Personal	General
9	4	

The first thirteen letters are traditionally ascribed to Paul, nine to churches and four to individuals. The order of the nine letters to the churches is not chronological but governed by other factors. The first is length, since Romans and 1 Corinthians are the two longest (sixteen chapters each), followed by 2 Corinthians (thirteen) and Galatians and Ephesians (six), with the rest all shorter.

Although not intended as such, they can also helpfully be arranged by topic. The first four letters are all concerned with faith, and centre on Christ and the cross. In Romans and Galatians the great reformed teaching on 'justification by faith through grace alone' is found. The Christian life begins when people put their trust completely in what Christ has done for them.

Although the Christian life is personal, it is never individualistic. God never calls us to be Christians in isolation, and the next three letters deal with the Christian in community. They focus on Christ and his church: where we are called to live, worship and serve. To live effectively as the people of God we need to love other Christians. Ephesians and Colossians also focus on the uniqueness of Christ.

> The Christian life begins when people put their trust completely in what Christ has done for them.

The final two, among the earliest written, are concerned with the future. They are concerned with Christ and his coming and are a call to hope.

6. Romans – the heart of the Christian faith– justification by faith (1:16–17)

Romans provides a great statement of the gospel. This has been called Paul's magnum opus. He refers at least seventy times to fourteen different Old Testament books. In many ways it unpacks Paul's experience on the Damascus road. It carefully demolishes our self-confidence and throws us onto the grace of God revealed in Jesus Christ. Paul recounts his testimony three times in Acts, once in Galatians and once in Philippians. In some ways he never moves beyond that in his ministry.

Whereas the other apostles came to learn about Jesus by sharing his life and ministry, then living through the horror of his death and the wonder of his resurrection, for Paul things happened in a different order. His faith began with the risen Christ. From there he was driven back to look afresh at the cross. Possibly only some years later, spending two weeks with Peter in Jerusalem, did he get fully briefed on the life and ministry of Jesus. That may explain, in part, why so much in his letters focuses on the death and resurrection of Jesus.

Its central thesis is found in Romans 1:16–17: 'I am not ashamed of the gospel, because it is the power of God for the salvation to everyone who believes: first to the Jew, then for the Gentile. For in the gospel a righteousness from God is revealed, a righteousness that is by faith from first to last, just as it is written: "The righteous will live by faith."'

Chapters 1–11 Gospel of salvation: doctrinal

a) Condemnation (1:18 – 3:20): the gospel needed
b) Salvation (3:21 – 8): the gospel message
   i)   3:21 – 5:11 – right with God
   ii) 5:12 – 8:11 – living by faith
   iii) 8:12–30 – our future hope
c) History (9–11): objections dealt with

Chapters 12–16 Transformation by salvation: practical

a) Problems of duty (12, 13)
   – in the church (12:1–13)
   – in the world (12:14–21)
   – as citizens (13)
b) Principles of action (14–15): Christian liberty, love, unity
c) Greetings (16)

We can get inside Romans best if we understand why it was written. Paul was writing to a church he had not started or ever visited, though he knew a good number of its members personally. In chapter 16 there are twenty-six names listed, two-thirds of whom are Gentiles. Paul was a master strategist. As Antioch had served him well as his eastern base, so now he needed to relocate to reach the west. He speaks in chapter 15 about longing to reach Spain for Christ. Spain was passing through one of its cultural highs at the time, with outstanding people like Seneca (prime minister to Nero) coming from it. It would not attain such a height again until the Middle Ages.

Romans is not Paul's systematic theology. There are aspects of Paul's beliefs that he does not mention here. Paul wanted to transform a local congregation into a world-conscious, mission-minded church, so it would become a staging post for the gospel – supporting it, praying for it and resourcing and serving it. He sought to enlarge their view of God and the gospel to achieve this. He wrote with burning logic to set their hearts on fire.

Paul ranges widely over all the types of people they might be expected to encounter in mission. There is the dissolute pagan, the moral person and the religious Jew. Whatever their background, their story or their knowledge, they all end up in the same place, silent before God, with no grounds for self-justification. Writing from Corinth, Paul knew the needs of the human heart and the depths it could plumb.

Into that dire situation steps God, who, in grace, takes the initiative. That is the force of the words in 3:21: 'But God...' His solution is shocking and radical: shocking because it involves God giving up his only Son to death; radical because it goes far beyond forgiveness to total transformation. Forgiveness is only the starting point on a road that leads to the renewal of our bodies. Salvation is comprehensive, dealing with past, present and future. It not only affects individuals but promises the renewal of the cosmos. Such a global vision that deals with geography – all the world – and history – all time – demands an unconditional response. That is the significance of the word 'Therefore' in chapter 12. Whenever you see the word 'therefore' you should ask 'What it is there for?' The implications of such commitment are not assumed, but our personal, social, civic and church responsibilities are carefully spelled out. Grasp this and the world becomes a global village.

> Paul wanted to transform a local congregation into a world-conscious, mission-minded church...

Paul's letters often split in two. The first part deals with doctrine and the second with practice. Christian doctrine is meant to be worked out, or the amassed knowledge puffs you up. Christian living is meant to be directed by the gospel otherwise it can easily become misdirected activity.

You can sense the passion with which Paul wrote from Gaius' home. Probably he was striding up and down as he dictated this to Tertius. The completed letter, wrapped in oilskin, was carried by Phoebe, a deacon, many miles from Corinth to Rome. There it would be read and for the last 2,000 years it has inspired, motivated and changed people and churches throughout the world.

7. First Letter to the Corinthians – working out the gospel – conduct (2:2)

Chapters 1–6 Correction following reports

a) Divisions (1–4)
b) Disorders
    – discipline
    – lawsuits
    – impurity

Chapters 7–16 Clarification following questions

    – difficulties and doctrine
    – marriage
    – liberty
    – holy living
      worship
    – communion
    – spiritual gifts
    – resurrection
    – giving

Paul's first letter to the Corinthians is written to a place where Paul lived during his second missionary journey. It was not easy living a distinctive Christian lifestyle in the cesspool of Corinth. This is a very practical letter dealing with specific concerns. Paul meets them head on in the first half. In the second half he clarifies other matters. Society's values were influencing the church's unity, worship and witness. The cross should change our perspective, values and attitudes. We need help to think it through and work it out.

Many people enjoy this letter because it is so practical. How many churches have known divisions over personalities and competing loyalties (chapters 1–4)? In a litigious culture, how common is it becoming for Christians to use the courts (chapter 6)? In a sexually confused society, what standards ought to operate for Christians (chapters 6–7)? How do you compare marriage and singleness? When do work ethics compromise faith (chapters 8–9)? Don't we still need help in worship and using spiritual gifts (chapters 10–14)? Certainly, few things are more divisive in a congregation. Do we not all need constant teaching about the priority of Christian love shown in selfless service (chapter 13)? In a here-and-now society, are we persuaded of the reality of life beyond death and the truth of the resurrection (chapter 15)? Finally, have we got good guidelines for Christian giving (chapter 16)?

> The cross should change our perspective, values and attitudes.

8. Second Letter to the Corinthians – workers for the gospel – ministry (4:10–12; 6:9)

Chapters 1–5   Paul's account of his ministry

- the minister explains
- his motive
- his ministry

Chapters 6–9   Paul's appeal to his converts

- the father encourages
a) Appeal (6–7)
b) Giving (8–9)

Chapters 10–13 Paul's answer to his critics

– the apostle justifies
a) Authority (10)
b) Apostleship (11–12)
c) Admonition (13)

The second letter of Paul to Corinth is intensely personal and passionate. A church he has planted has listened to other voices that want to supplant his authority. His ministry has been subjected to revision and largely dismissed.

While such treatment hurts, and Paul was intensely human, this was more than a takeover bid. It involved changing the gospel itself and so could not go uncontested. The usurpers were Judaizers wanting to bring the people back under bondage to the Jewish law and traditions. Legalists can look spiritual and holy, but they end up enslaving those who listen. He defends his ministry in a remarkably frank autobiographical way. He lifts the lid on the so-called romance of leadership, and spells out the costliness of preaching the cross.

> Legalists can look spiritual and holy, but they end up enslaving those who listen.

This letter fills in a number of important details in Paul's ministry. Here we read about his thorn in the flesh (chapter 12). In the list of sufferings (chapter 11) he recounts a number that are not included in Acts. They must have happened during one of those periods in Paul's life about which Acts is silent. For instance, he spent about nine years in Tarsus before going to Antioch. Did his scourging and shipwrecks happen then?

There are wonderful passages about what true Christian ministry involves (chapters 4–6) and how we should approach the way we give (chapters 8–9). But throughout the book the pain the apostle felt is almost tangible, and it makes a sober read. To make the gospel known, Paul had spilt his blood. There was a cross in Paul's life as there should be in the life of all who serve Jesus. Jesus said, 'Whoever wants to be my disciple must deny themselves and take up their cross daily and follow me' (Luke 9:23). Paul simply took him at his word.

9. Galatians – defence of the gospel – set free to serve (2:20)

Chapters 1–2 Authenticity of the gospel – personal

- Paul's authority defended – apology
- genuine as to its origin
- genuine as to its nature

Chapters 3–4 Superiority of the gospel – doctrinal

- Paul's gospel declared – argument

Chapters 5–6 True liberty of the gospel – practical

- Paul's faith demands – appeal

After the sorrow in 2 Corinthians, the tone of Galatians is passionate anger. No one could ever accuse Paul of indifference! Paul is fighting for the life of the gospel against those who would destroy it. Individuals and congregations were turning from the gospel, thinking they were growing in maturity by doing so. These were places and people Paul knew, and he fought for the truth. The gospel had set them free and now he saw them trading in that freedom for a new form of slavery. His core belief was this: 'I have been crucified with Christ and I no longer live, but Christ lives in me. The life I now live in the body, I live by faith in the Son of God, who loved me and gave himself for me' (2:20).

Paul is quite clear. There is only one gospel. Any alternative is to be resisted and those teaching it should be cursed. He makes a frank statement of his apostolic authority by telling of his conversion. He recounts incidents that helped shape his understanding in the early days, later ratified by the Jerusalem apostles (1–2). In fact, he even rebuked Peter when, with Barnabas, Peter was led astray into inconsistent living. They had been persuaded not to eat with Gentile Christians. It took a public intervention by Paul to rectify the situation. He takes on the false teachers directly by appealing to the Old Testament. He focuses on Abraham, the father of the faith, and by speaking both of circumcision (the contentious issue) and of the law, he exposes the flaws in their thinking.

It is time to change direction. He appeals to them to forsake wrong living and to display the fragrant ninefold fruit of the Spirit, to take their stand in the crucified community of faith. We must each make a choice between faith and works, gospel and law, the Spirit and the flesh. Martin Luther said that a Christian is at one and the same time the freest of all and the servant of all. But then Christian service is perfect freedom when you have such a master as Christ. The choice we must make is not between legalism and licence but for liberty – we are free in Christ, set free to serve.

> There is only one gospel. Any alternative is to be resisted and those teaching it should be cursed.

10. Ephesians – Christ in the church – glory (4:13)

Chapters 1–3 Our wealth in Christ – the church's heavenly calling – doctrinal

a) Praise for spiritual possessions (1)
   – prayer for spiritual perception
b) New condition in Christ (2)
   – new relations in Christ
c) Revealing divine mystery (3)
   – receiving divine fullness

Chapters 4–6 Our walk in Christ – the church's earthly conduct – practice

a) Church (4:1–16)
b) Conduct (4:17 – 6:9)
c) Conflict (6:10–20)

The letter to the Ephesians begins the second section of Paul's church letters, and has been called the Queen of all Epistles. There is little local colouring. It may well have been a circular letter to Ephesus and neighbouring churches. Some say this is the height of Paul's devotional writings. Here, Christ's church is set forth in all its splendour as Christ's building, Christ's body and Christ's bride. The letter divides naturally, with chapters 1–3 dealing with doctrine and 4–6 with application: what we believe and how we behave. Firstly, he tells us what Christ has done for us and then spells out what we are called to do for Christ.

The writer begins by reminding us of all we have received in Christ. So moved is he that he bursts out in praise. Most of chapter 1:3–13 is one unbroken sentence. The blessings we have in Christ tumble over one another. These are followed by a prayer of longing, that we might experience all God wants to give us.

He recounts the difference Christ has made. Without Christ we were stateless, homeless, hopeless, Christless and Godless. Then that little word that changes everything: 'But God ...', which means 'something has happened to change the situation – good news, or gospel'. This gospel not only produces radical personal change, but breaks down the barriers that divide humanity, supremely the barrier between Jew and Gentile, but also that between male and female, slave and free.

> Christ's church is set forth in all its splendour as Christ's building, Christ's body and Christ's bride.

God's new rainbow community challenges all social stereotypes including all ages, backgrounds, types and experiences, united in Christ Jesus. A new community needs a new lifestyle. New living requires new energy and guidance, and Christians are called to go on being filled with the Holy Spirit to make this possible. Paul details its implications, first for the worship of God, and then how it affects marriage, family life and daily work. Being filled with the Spirit is primarily about a moral, not a mystical, change.

The great picture of the soldier and his armour (chapter 6:10–20) makes sense only if the soldier is part of an army. While each of us is responsible for putting on the whole armour of God and being aware of the chinks in our own armour, we are called to stand together and to take mutual responsibility for each other. We can become so preoccupied with personal holiness that we forget the call to build up the church of God.

11. Philippians –
Christians in Christ – joy (1:21)

Chapter 1 Experience

  – Christ our life

Chapters 2–3 Exposition

  – Christ our mind (2)
  – Christ our goal (3)

Chapter 4 Exhortation

  – Christ our strength

This little letter is full of joy because it is full of Jesus. The two go together. The story of the beginning of this church is told graphically in Acts 16. The three conversions related there have added humour when you remember that Paul, when still Saul the Pharisee, would have prayed daily, 'Lord, I thank you that I am not a slave, a woman or a Gentile' – for these three groupings made up the Philippian church! Paul confronted a Greek slave girl who had the right theology but the wrong spirit, and set her free from her obsession. He saw a middle-class Roman jailer, a Gentile, quake with fear when he recognized the power of Paul's God, and seek salvation for himself and his household. First of all the converts, though, was a woman, who came quietly to Christ. Lydia, an upper-class Asian trader, listened to Paul by the banks of the River Gangites (now known as the Zygakte) and the Lord opened her heart. She, in turn, opened her home to the apostolic party.

Now Paul writes to encourage them. He is in prison but not by God's will. He sees his chains as an opportunity to witness to the crack praetorian guard. Instead of saying 'Poor me, I'm chained', he could say 'Poor jailer, he's chained to me!' He had a captive audience, and, once he started speaking, he sparked off a chain reaction! Paul was quite clear where his priorities lay, whatever he faced. 'For to me, to live is Christ and to die is gain' (1:21). This is not a bad philosophy to live by, and a wonderful truth to die for.

He establishes the basis for Christian unity and the importance of working together. This requires a right spirit and attitude. Supremely, this is seen in Christ's humility and obedience in the face of the cross. However, it also was demonstrated by the servant spirit of Timothy and Epaphroditus.

> 'For to me, to live is Christ and to die is gain' (1:21). This is not a bad philosophy to live by, and a wonderful truth to die for.

Paul tells of his background and conversion to show how foolish it is to try to earn salvation. He warns of the twin perils of legalism and licence. He reveals a great hunger to know Christ better and a burning ambition to become more like him.

Christlikeness starts in the mind. Paul contrasts two squabbling women with a spirit of prayer and a mind filled with good and wholesome things. Here is the way to find Christian contentment whatever the circumstances.

12. Colossians – God in Christ, Christ in us – fullness (2:9–10)

Chapters 1–2 Christ the fullness of God

- that you may be filled – doctrinal
a) Person and work of Christ
- in creation
- in redemption
- in the church

Chapters 3–4   Practice of indwelling of Christ

- that you may walk worthily – practical

a) Spiritual principles for inner life (3:1–17)
b) Special precepts for outer life (3:18 – 4:6)

The last letter in this section is Colossians, which is similar to Ephesians except in tone. In fact, seventy-eight out of ninety-five verses have a marked resemblance to Ephesians. But Paul writes to combat false teaching rather than to state Christian truth. This letter gives us a big view of Christ. Christ is the fullness of God, active in creation, central in redemption and head of the church.

Remarkably, Christ, the fullness of God, dwells in us, giving us the hope of glory. If so, then in Christ we have all we need. 'So then, just as you received Christ Jesus as Lord, continue to live your lives in him, rooted and built up in him, strengthened in the faith as you were taught, and overflowing with thankfulness' (2:6–7). He warns against those who mislead. We are to think through and work out what the Christian life will look like in practice.

Paul uses a vivid picture of changing clothes, exchanging old clothes for new. New clothes feel different. We take time and effort and go to some expense to dress up for an occasion. You don't spoil a new outfit by keeping some old clothes (even hat, bag and shoes apparently have to change!). So, to live the Christian life, former attitudes must go and new values take over. This is not just a makeover, it is transformation.

When speaking to the Ephesian church (chapter 4), Paul says that we are Christ's body. Here the emphasis is on Christ being our head. In Ephesians he says, 'Be filled with the Spirit'; here in the parallel passage he says, 'Let the word of Christ dwell in you richly.' The two hold together, word and Spirit, for the Spirit moved people to write God's word and opens our eyes and minds to understand it. It is often when we are reading and living God's word that we are most aware of being filled with the Spirit. We need both God's word and God's Spirit to make a go of marriage, family life and daily work.

> Christ is the fullness of God, active in creation, central in redemption and head of the church.

13. First Letter to the Thessalonians – new converts encouraged – coming (1:3, 9, 10)

Chapters 1–3 Looking back – how they were saved

– reminiscent
a) Exemplary conversion (1)
b) Exemplary evangelism (2)
c) Exemplary aftercare (3)

Chapters 4–5 Looking on – how they should live

– practical
a) Conduct and calling in the light of the Father's will (4:1–12)
b) Comfort and challenge in the prospect of Lord's return (4:13 – 5:11)
c) Concord and constancy in keeping with Christian fellowship (5:12–24)
d) Requests and benediction (5:25–28)

> The church grew and faced persecution but remained faithful and persevering throughout, loving and united.

Paul's final two letters to churches are to the Christians in Thessalonica. These may be among the first letters Paul wrote. He looks back, remembering how the first Christians there came to faith. He talks in chapter 1 verse 3 about their work of faith, their labour of love and the hope that endures. Not bad consequences for a mission that may have lasted only three weeks (Acts 17)! No wonder he rejoiced when Timothy returned with a good report on their progress.

In chapter 2 we see how evangelism should be undertaken. Paul describes, in a vivid series of word pictures, how you need to be as courageous as a soldier, as humble as a servant, as tender as a mother, as strong as a father and as devoted as a lover.

We read of his continuing concern in prayer and of the thorough follow-up once he left. The church grew and faced persecution but remained faithful and persevering throughout, loving and united.

He tells them how they should live in the light of Christ's coming. The truth of Christ's return is not to feed our curiosity but to deepen our commitment. His coming is certain but its timing is unknown, so we should always be ready. Some were using the expectation of his imminent return as an excuse for idleness, and Paul pulls them up sharply. Because the future is sure, we can face the present with quiet faith and courage.

14. Second Letter to the Thessalonians – live in the light of his return – work and wait (2:14)

Chapter 1 Comfort from the hope of Christ's return

– inspiration for the oppressed

Chapter 2 Caution on the time for Christ's return

– instruction for the perplexed

Chapter 3 Command in the light of Christ's return

– injunction for the disorderly

Paul's final letter to the churches is this short sequel. The early church didn't always grasp first time what they were taught. If his first letter was to comfort, this more severe one corrects.

Either they had not grasped what Paul had said or someone had twisted his words. Paul reminded them that they were to be faithful whatever they were doing. Never get tired of doing what is right. That is as valid today as when it was first written.

So we conclude Paul's nine church letters. As we remember what Christ has done for us on the cross, we trust him as our saviour and

> Paul reminded them that they were to be faithful whatever they were doing. Never get tired of doing what is right.

Lord. Looking at what Christ is doing, building his church, we must shine as lights, serve in Christ's name and worship and witness to his glory. Finally, we believe that history is neither pointless nor circular. It has a beginning and a destination. So we look forward in hope to Christ's coming again. Hallelujah!

Paul's four letters to individuals

In these personal letters Paul encourages those who would carry on the work after him. Not only was Paul a great leader, but he developed leadership in others. He delegated responsibility to bring out the best in others. He trained and trusted the next generation (2 Timothy 2:2). One strategy was to mentor others. People such as Silas, Timothy and Titus benefited from his care and support. The gospel was not for one generation only, so he prepared for succeeding generations. The Psalmist said, 'We will tell the next generation.' That was Paul's practice. Fail to do that and you weaken the church in its mission.

Timothy came from Lystra, and had a Jewish mother and a Gentile father. He became a Christian during Paul's first missionary journey. As Timothy watched (or heard about) Paul being stoned and left for dead in his own home town, he had no illusions about the cost of following Christ.

He met Paul again during Paul's second missionary journey, and became his special companion. They blended well: the older man sharing his experience and vision; the younger, a faithful lieutenant, drinking in his wisdom and learning from him.

Timothy had been given leadership of the church at Ephesus, a church Paul knew well. Paul wrote from Rome under house arrest in a hired house. By the time Paul wrote his second letter to Timothy (the last he wrote), he was in a dungeon awaiting execution.

After being under house arrest, Paul was released. A few years later he was arrested again, probably as part of Nero's persecution of the Christians (his selected scapegoat for the great fire of Rome). From his dungeon, tradition says, Paul was executed with a Roman sword.

We call the two letters to Timothy and the one to Titus pastoral letters, because they are concerned with ministry. Those called to minister God's word must equip the church for service.

15. First Letter to Timothy – the local church and its minister – faithfulness (6:12)

Chapters 1–3 Church of God – Timothy's charge

a) Church and people – doctrine
   – her gospel, the faith (1)
b) Church and God – devotion
   – her intercession: the worship (2)
c) Church and herself – duties
   – her leadership and their roles: the oversight (3)
   – elders
   – deacons

Chapters 4–6 Charge to Timothy – the ministry

a) His walk – personal – walk with God
   – duty towards the truth (4)
b) His work– official – witness for God
   – duty towards his flock (5)
   – older, younger, widows, elders
   – duty towards himself (6)

Paul's two great themes are God's church and Timothy's charge. Paul shows how the church should be organized. He then explains how Timothy's calling should work out. He will say similar things about the church to Titus and more things about Timothy's calling in 2 Timothy.

You could helpfully read 1 Timothy 1–3 alongside Titus as a kind of minister's manual, and 1 Timothy 4–6 alongside 2 Timothy. Paul wants to ensure that the church is true to what it believes. Jesus is supreme, the only one who has dealt with sin, brought new life and given us hope.

In the second chapter he speaks about worship and prayer in church. In chapter 3 he lays down criteria for appointing leaders, both elders and deacons. Leadership is based on Christian character and commitment, not on social status or power.

Timothy needs to be helped to rise to the challenge. He was comparatively young, shy, sensitive, not robust in health or naturally charismatic in character. He must walk close to the Lord and be clear about his faith. Then he can take his responsibilities seriously.

He must ensure that the vulnerable are properly looked after. Paul gives clear guidance about caring for widows, and also on the part families should play. Younger widows should be treated differently, as some might choose remarriage.

> Leadership is based on Christian character and commitment, not on social status or power.

Paul warns Timothy that he should expect difficulties from false teachers and distractions from the love of money. He lists some things that Timothy should flee from, follow and fight. It will be hard and will require God's grace.

16. Second Letter to Timothy – final words – passing the torch – guard the gospel (2:2)

Chapters 1–2 Personal equipment for the ministry

a) Essential qualities in suffering – gifts (1)
b) Necessary discipline for service – grace (2)

Chapters 3–4 Public fulfilment of the ministry

a) The coming change – trust God's word (3)
b) The closing charge – do God's will (4)

This is Paul's last letter, and reads like a last will and testament. It is hard to read it without a mist coming over your eyes. Paul is alone, partly because he kept sending everyone away to comfort others. He is cold, missing his manuscripts, and longing for news and company. He fears that his work is unravelling and that, as it gets harder to be a Christian, fewer will pay that price. If the church fails, then truth will be silenced.

What a need to stand up and be counted. Therefore they must be clear about the gospel, strengthened by the Spirit and willing to suffer.

Timothy, who was not a natural leader, needed to be reminded of his own spiritual history. He had not been given a spirit of timidity but a spirit of power and love and self-control. Paul presents a whole series of word pictures of a Christian worker: a growing child, a faithful teacher, a hardy soldier, a keen athlete, a successful farmer, an unashamed workman and a clean vessel. Paul has handed to Timothy work that was entrusted to him by the risen Lord Jesus. Timothy must guard that truth and pass it on to those who will teach others also.

> If the church fails, then truth will be silenced. Therefore they must be clear about the gospel, strengthened by the Spirit and willing to suffer.

Finally, alone and imprisoned, Paul is clear that his work is over. He has fought the fight, run the race and completed the course. Ahead lies reward and the 'Well done' of his master. It is great when someone not only starts but finishes well. Paul will get his well-deserved reward.

17. Titus – reforming church life – behaviour (2:11, 12)

Chapter 1 Rule of the church – minister

– character and conduct – order

Chapter 2 Walk of the church – message

– content and authority – behaviour

Chapter 3 State and the church – members

– to others and to God – relationships

Titus is never mentioned in Acts. All we know about him comes from Paul's letters, yet that is enough. He was an uncircumcized Gentile, one of Paul's converts, and an occasional travelling companion. Titus is a strong but sympathetic character. He is able to make a stand.

He has been given temporary responsibility for the church in Crete. Cretans had an unenviable reputation. Titus was building a church of those who would live distinctly different lives.

The leaders need to set an example. First, look at their personal and family life. Then consider their specific skills of leadership and teaching. If there are weaknesses at a personal or family level these will undermine their ministry.

> If there are weaknesses at a personal or family level these will undermine their ministry.

If the church receives the gospel then change is inevitable. So Paul explains how the gospel will affect them both as citizens and as Christians. We have responsibilities to society and to God. There is a final encouragement to do what is good. Greetings and grace conclude this letter.

18. Philemon –
slave and brother – practical Christianity
(20)

Verses 1–7 Paul's praise of Philemon

– commendation

Verses 8–17 Paul's plea for Onesimus

– supplication

Verses 18–22 Paul's pledge and assurance

– expectation

Paul's final personal letter probably went with the circular letters to Ephesus and Colossae. Addressed to Philemon, it concerned a private though not a trivial matter. It shows how love works out in practice. Philemon, a wealthy leader in the Colossian church, had a slave called Onesimus, who had run away and probably stolen something to see him on his way. Onesimus crossed Asia Minor and headed for Rome, where he hoped to start a new life. Somehow the slave met Paul and was converted. What should he do now to sort out his past?

Paul writes with courtesy, delicacy and tact. He could, with apostolic authority, have told Philemon what he wanted to be done. Instead, he writes as a brother, praising Philemon for his Christian character. He then begs Philemon to receive Onesimus back and not to punish him. Paul will stand as guarantor for Onesimus. This 'useless slave' has become useful to Paul. He pleads his case in the letter carried by Tychicus, who accompanies Onesimus home and who will act as Paul's mediator.

Paul also commends Onesimus to the church so that they will see that the right action is taken. In this short letter you see love controlling relationships. Paul asks Philemon to treat Onesimus as a Christian brother, not just as a fugitive slave. Paul would have liked to retain Onesimus as a personal attendant and Philemon, no doubt, would have liked to punish the runaway, but it was not to be.

It would have been easy for Paul to say that the slave's past did not matter, but it did. It had to be faced up to by both of them. No doubt when Onesimus and Philemon met there would have been a sticky moment or two, but love endures all things and is kind. The message to the church was that love never fails.

> The message to the church was that love never fails.

It is a short but a good letter. In this letter ideas were planted like a time bomb that centuries later would explode, bringing about the end of slavery. Slavery could not be attacked directly, at that stage, without such opinions being ruthlessly suppressed. But when a slave is no longer seen as a thing but as a person, not a living tool but a human being, a brother with a name and a story, then, in that society at least, the future of slavery is doomed.

We now move away from Paul's letters to look at letters written by others. Unlike Paul's letters, these do not have a clear context. We have little idea of where they went. Some, no doubt, were circular letters and went from congregation to congregation. These letters were mainly addressed to Jewish converts to Christianity and so are filled with Old Testament references, pictures and illustrations, making them harder for us. Yet they are marvellous letters, a real inspiration.

19. Hebrews – superiority of Christ – far better (12:1, 2)

Chapters 1–7   Jesus, the new and better deliverer

a) Jesus the god–man
    – better than angels (1–2)
b) Jesus the new apostle and leader
    – better than Moses and Joshua (3–4)
c) Jesus the new priest like Melchizedek
    – better than Aaron (5–7)

Chapters 8–10 Calvary, the new and better covenant

a) New covenant has better promises (8)
b) New covenant opens up a better sanctuary (9:1–14)
c) New covenant is sealed by a better sacrifice (9:15–28)
d) New covenant achieves far better results (10:1–18)

Chapters 10:19 – 13 Faith, the true and better principle

a) Faith the true response to those better things (10:19–39)
b) Faith has always been vindicated as such (11)
c) Faith is now to endure patiently, looking to Jesus (12:1–13)
d) Faith is now to express itself in practical holiness (12:14 – 13:21)

We have no idea who wrote the letter to the Hebrews. Was it Apollos, or Barnabas, or perhaps even a woman? It was written to proclaim the greatness and the humanity of Jesus. Here we see Jesus struggling with temptation, understanding what we face. Yet he fought and won, choosing to do what was right, obeying his Father's will. Having triumphed, he can help us if we trust him.

This letter is written to Jews who were finding being Christians hard going. They had left so much behind. Important places were no longer central; familiar rituals had been left behind. The temptation, when persecution came, was to revert in nostalgia to the safe, familiar world of Temple, priest and sacrifice, their natural default position.

Do not go back, urges the writer, because Jesus is far better. He is a better mediator than the angels. They are servants; Jesus is God's Son. Jesus is a better leader than Moses or Joshua. Moses could get the people out of Egypt but he could not get Egypt out of the people. Joshua could get the people into the land but there followed generations of struggle and conflict. They never truly found rest. Jesus sets people free from the supreme slavery of sin, and guarantees our final rest. His work was completed; no more needed to be done.

Priests and sacrifices were impressive, but their work was never finished. Every day, sacrifices had to be offered. Even the priest was flawed, having to offer sacrifices for himself before he could offer them for others. Jesus is far better. He never sinned, so did not need to offer sacrifices for himself. Jesus came from a better priestly line, not from Aaron but from Melchizedek.

> It was written to proclaim the greatness and the humanity of Jesus.

Melchizedek appears suddenly in the Old Testament with no mention of his origin or of what happened to him, beyond his one encounter with Abraham. He was a priest–king. Abraham recognized him and deferred to him. Since Aaron was descended from Abraham through Levi, effectively Aaron also submitted to Melchizedek. Now, says the writer, Jesus is like Melchizedek. He has no beginning and no end. He too is a priest–king. He is a better priest than Aaron.

Jesus offers a better sacrifice. Although care was taken to offer a lamb without blemish, in the end it was still simply a lamb. Jesus came as the Lamb of God, and offered himself, once for all, as a sacrifice for sin. That offering having been accepted, no further sacrifices are needed.

The place where people met God was firstly the tabernacle and later the Temple. Impressive as they were, with beautiful proportions and costly building materials, both were limited. For strict limits were laid down on how close anyone could come. Non-Jews were restricted to the court of the Gentiles, women to the court of the women. Jewish men had limits placed on them, and priests were not able to go beyond the holy place. Only the great high priest (and that only on the Day of Atonement) could go into the holy of holies, where the ark of the covenant was kept.

Jesus came to make access to God available to all, at all times. That was why, when Jesus died, the veil of the Temple was torn in two from top to bottom. Jew or Gentile, male or female, ordained or lay, could now draw near to God anywhere, anytime. Jesus provided a new and living way into the very presence of God!

> **Jesus came to make access to God available to all, at all times.**

The Jews rejoiced that they were the covenant people of God, their identity being found in the covenants made with Abraham, Moses and David. Jesus came to implement Jeremiah's new covenant (Jeremiah 31), whereby forgiveness is offered fully and freely, even for deliberate disobedience. Then the law of God would be written not just in words to be learned, but on our hearts. We will desire to keep the law not because we have to, but, because we want to. What a difference that makes.

The great figures in the Old Testament lived their lives trusting in God's word. They believed God's promises. Many of them never saw the outcome of their belief, but they still trusted. We too are called to live by faith in God's promises. The difference, however, is that Jesus has come. We look back to his life, death and resurrection and draw our strength from them.

With such a gospel it would be disastrous to turn back now, the writer argues. Join that great cloud of witnesses and, looking to Jesus, keep on keeping on. Not that life will be easy, or deliverance will inevitably come. In chapter 11 the writer, without qualification, speaks of some who by faith escaped death by the sword while others, also living by faith, died by the sword! It is not the outcome but the attitude that matters.

There are a number of passages of encouragement that begin 'Let us' that still inspire and challenge today. There also serious warnings not to slip back, or turn away or depart the faith. These must be taken seriously, not dismissed merely as rhetoric. The last three chapters are a call to faith (11), to hope (12), and to love (13), a great way to conclude.

The last seven letters, sometimes called the General Letters, are written by two apostles, Peter (two) and John (three), and two family members of Jesus, James and Jude.

20. James – the tests of faith – working faith (2:26)

Chapter 1 Faith leads to victory in temptation

– it endures trials and testing

Chapter 2 Faith leads to service to others

– it is good towards all
– to the poor: impartiality
– to the needy: generosity

Chapter 3 Faith leads to wisdom in speech

– it controls the tongue

Chapter 4 Faith leads to purity in character

– it seeks godliness in all things

Chapter 5 Faith leads to hope

– it faces all situations bravely

This James is not John's brother, but Jesus'. He came to faith after the resurrection. Paul tells us that Jesus appeared to James (1 Corinthians

15:7). He became the leader of the church in Jerusalem, and was concerned to show how our faith works out in practice. He had a great reputation for prayer. It was said that his knees were calloused like a camel's.

James is a wonderfully searching letter, even if Luther called it an 'epistle of straw'. Luther was concerned that nothing should cloud the doctrine of justification by faith. So the mention of justification by works (2:24) set all his alarm bells going. He wasn't going to lose the new freedom he had found in Christ.

But James and Paul do not contradict each other. They are writing to different audiences for different purposes. Paul is writing to those who are still trying to get right with God by what they do, either through their religious rituals or by their moral earnestness. That way will never lead to God because you can never be good enough, all the time, to everyone. Our trust must be in Christ alone. There is no other way.

James is writing to Christians who were in danger of using their professed faith in Christ to opt out of living changed lives. Christianity is not about a magic formula – speak certain words and all is well. Words must spring from a sincere heart, and, if so, faith will never stop at words. Thankful hearts will express themselves in action and in Christian service. So show your faith. Paul says in Ephesians 2:8–9: 'For it is by grace you have been saved, through faith – and this not from yourselves, it is the gift of God – not by works, so that no-one can boast'. But then he continues (verse 10): 'For we are God's workmanship, created in Christ Jesus to do good works, which God prepared in advance for us to do.'

'We are just before God by faith, just before people by works, just by the works of faith, just by the faith that works'.

> Christianity is not about a magic formula – speak certain words and all is well. Words must spring from a sincere heart, and, if so, faith will never stop at words. Thankful hearts will express themselves in action and in Christian service.

There are similarities between this letter and the wisdom literature. James deals with how Christians ought to live, both in good times and in bad. He knew that we could talk the talk without necessarily walking the walk .He knew how vicious Christian tongues could be. So he addresses a variety of practical issues. Mark Twain said, 'It is not the parts of the Bible I do not understand I have trouble with, but the parts I do!' This is not difficult to understand but it is difficult to live. He prepares us for facing trials and temptations (chapter 1), and warns against favouritism and of empty words (chapter 2), the perils of the tongue (chapter 3) a right spirit to others and God. He speaks against fighting, boasting and covetousness (chapter 4). He encourages true humility shown in patience and prayer (chapter 5) and love to those in need.

If Paul is noted for faith and James for action, then Peter calls us to hope and John to love. If Paul stands for Christian freedom and James for Christian living, then Peter urges steadfastness through trials, and John stresses real Christian experience. We need all these insights to live a rounded Christian life.

21. First Letter of Peter – Christ our strength in suffering – example (2:21)

Chapters 1 – 2:10 The living hope

- the Christian's vocation
- salvation

Chapters 2:11 – 3 The pilgrim life

- the Christian's behaviour
- submission

Chapters 4–5 The fiery trial

- the Christian's discipline
- suffering

Troubles from outside the church

We turn to the first of Peter's two letters. Peter is one of the most loved biblical characters, whose faith development we trace in the gospels, and growth to maturity we see in Acts.

There is an interesting balance. The first letter of Peter is concerned with troubles that come to the church from outside, especially through persecution. His second letter is concerned with troubles that come to a church from inside, through false teaching. Such teaching cuts the nerve of Christian faith and imperils Christian living.

In both these letters Peter wants us to recognize that Christ is our strength. The promise given to Paul, 'My grace is sufficient for you' (2 Corinthians 12:9), applies here also. Peter holds up to the toiling church the example of Jesus, our mighty saviour and victorious sufferer. He makes it clear what our living hope is when life is bleak. In chapter 1 he shows how salvation reaches back into the past, touches us in the present and prepares us for a secure future. Then in chapter 2 he speaks of the strength we can draw from the church, where we have a part to play as living stones in God's Temple. Because our future is settled we can accept being pilgrim people just now and forsake present security.

To fulfil God's purpose we must not just to *do* something, we need to *become* something, and that will affect our behaviour and our relationships. We will sometimes have to go against society's trends and not be universally popular. Christian witness often leads to facing fiery trials, but Christ will be with us, having faced them first. He is able to take us through and, at the end, bring us safely home.

22. Second Letter of Peter – troubles from within – knowledge (3:18)

Chapter 1 The true knowledge in which to grow

– plan for holy living

Chapter 2 The false teachers who were to come

– possibility of unholy living

Chapter 3 The sure promise to give us hope

– persevere, for he is coming again

Troubles from inside the church

The second letter of Peter is very different in form. Parts of chapter 2 read very like the letter of Jude. To combat wrong thinking and wrong teaching you need to grow in your Christian faith. Some, never maturing, remain content with a childish faith, which leaves them vulnerable to wrong teaching. To be effective we need to be clear who Jesus is, and what that means.

Although Peter had experienced Jesus' transfiguration he pointed beyond that to God's revelation in scripture, as people moved by the Holy Spirit wrote from God (1:21). The Bible is a key resource in helping us to grow.

Peter speaks forcibly about false teachers, where they come from, what they teach, and their impact. We can easily be led astray by the appearance of spirituality or by smooth words, convincingly presented. We must be alert and see that such teaching leads to destruction, not life.

> ... Peter shows that the return of Christ, often laughed at and dismissed, still remains the certain Christian hope. If he is coming again, and he is, start preparing now.

In his final chapter Peter shows that the return of Christ, often laughed at and dismissed, still remains the certain Christian hope. If he is coming again, and he is, start preparing now.

23. The Three Letters of John

The First Letter of John – walking in the light – assurance (5:13)

Chapters 1–2 Fellowship with God in light

– forgiveness and growth

Chapters 3–4 Fellowship with God in love

– action and attitude

Chapter 5 Fellowship with God in life

– saved to serve

Now we turn to the apostle John's three letters, two of which are very short. We already have the Gospel ascribed to John, and later his Revelation. If Peter founded the early church and Paul emancipated it, then John established it. John was one of Jesus' inner three, with Peter and James (his martyred brother). Referred to as 'the disciple whom Jesus loved', he sat next to him during the last supper. He, alone among the apostles, was present at the cross, comforting Jesus' mother and becoming responsible for her. Jesus changed him, from one of the 'sons of thunder' to the 'apostle of love'. He was at the forefront of the early church's struggles, appearing before the Sanhedrin with Peter (Acts 4). The last of the apostles to die, he alone, according to tradition, died a natural death. Exiled on the Isle of Patmos, he later retired to Ephesus, where he was held in high regard.

Two stories remain of him. He was in the bathhouse when a false teacher called Cerinthus came in. John, horrified, wrapped himself in his bath towel and rushed out!

When asked to give a message to the church he simply said, 'Little children, love one another.' A short time later, when asked again, he repeated this message. When this happened a third time, one of them explained that they had heard that message already. He replied, 'Little children, if you love one another then that is the heart of the Christian message!' If ministers preached new sermons only when the previous one was acted upon, far fewer sermons would be written!

As with his gospel (John 20:30–31), John helpfully states the purpose of the letter (5:13): 'I write these things to you who believe in the name of the Son of God so that you may know that you have eternal life.' His Gospel was written to tell us what happened, in sufficient detail that we might put our faith in Jesus Christ. Here he writes to give us assurance that we are children of God.

He does so by outlining various tests of faith. Before that he urges us not to cover up wrongdoing, but to come clean. Then we can see how completely we are forgiven through Jesus (chapter 1).

> 'Little children, if you love one another then that is the heart of the Christian message!'

Being forgiven sets us free to grow in faith and serve others. Our love for God will be shown in our desire to know God better, our willingness to contend against evil, and our love for others. We will turn from sin and seek forgiveness when we fail. We will be discerning about what we hear, and will grow to appreciate all God has done for us in Christ. We will bring our faith to every situation and desire to help others grow and recover from failures. These are the marks of God's children.

The Second Letter of John – walk in his will – obedience (6)

Verses 1–6 Path of the believer – walk in love

– practical aspect

Verses 7–14 Peril of the believer – watch against error

– doctrinal aspect

What John teaches in 1 John, he illustrates in the next two little letters. Both deal with hospitality, one restricting it and the other encouraging it. His second letter warns against accepting those who will lead your church astray. In the third, John encourages us to have an open-door policy for servants of Christ.

> Walk in love and watch against error. Love needs to be strengthened by truth to avoid sentimentality. Truth needs to be softened by love to avoid harshness. Jesus was full of both love and truth.

The 'chosen lady and her children' may refer to a local church or to a Christian family. Its message is clear. Walk in love and watch against error. Love needs to be strengthened by truth to avoid sentimentality. Truth needs to be softened by love to avoid harshness. Jesus was full of both love and truth.

The Third Letter of John – walk in the truth – discernment (3)

Verses 1–11 Gaius – love practised

– confirmation

Verses 9–10 Diotrephes – love violated

– condemnation

Verses 11–14 Demetrius – love, light, life

– commendation

The third letter of John provides three interesting case studies. Firstly there is Gaius, who practised hospitality. Food adds an extra dimension to any occasion. In a lonely world, food helps people to feel included. The gift of hospitality is a wonderful one.

Diotrophes is far less attractive. He was arrogant, and enjoyed power. He dismissed John's letters because 'he loved to be first'! He started a whispering campaign to undermine John's authority and threw out any who disagreed. He stands condemned.

Finally, John writes a glowing, if brief, CV for Demetrius as an example of love, light and life.

24. Jude –
stand firm for the truth – contend (3)

Verses 1–16 Why to contend

- apostate teachers
- the danger

Verses 17–25 How to contend

- our true resources
- our duty

Jude is a short letter full of Old Testament allusions. Whatever his original intention in writing, his ultimate purpose is made clear in verse 3: 'I felt I had to write and urge you to contend for the faith that was once and for all entrusted to the saints.'

Jude, Jesus' brother, preferred to describe himself as a servant of Jesus and a brother of James. His letter bears many similarities to 2 Peter 2.

Jude is poetic and writes vividly. He ranges through history to warn, from experience, of the consequences of drifting from faith. False teaching lures people into wrong belief and wrong behaviour. He reminds them of the wasted wilderness years of murmuring following the exodus. He goes back to the original rebellion of the angels and the judgement of Sodom and Gomorrah. He reminds them of the fate of Cain, the error of Balaam and the rebellion of Korah. Numbers is a particularly fruitful source of his illustrations. He piles up images to show the emptiness of such teaching and the bankruptcy of those who advocate it.

They were warned this would happen, and should act now. Grow up, stand firm, and pray, trusting in Christ's mercy to deliver them from the peril they faced.

He concludes by affirming confidence in God, finishing with a great doxology of hope. It is not a cheery letter but it gives a salutary warning.

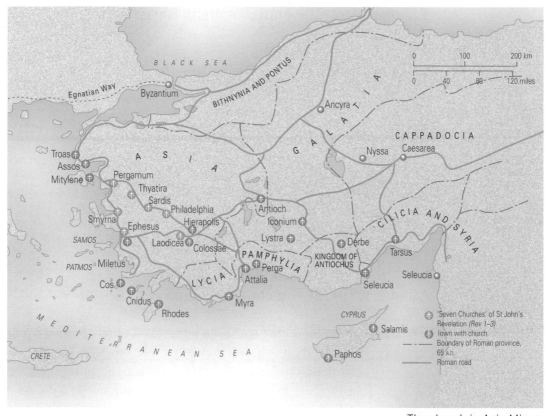

The church in Asia Minor

25. Revelation –
Christ and his church in conflict with
many foes – victory (1:18)

Chapters 1–3 The church's life in Christ

Chapters 4–6 The church's safety through Christ

Chapters 8–11 The church's witness to Christ

Chapters 12–14 The church's conflict for Christ

Chapters 15–20 The church's vindication by Christ

Chapters 21–22 The church's union with Christ

We have finally come to the last book of the Bible. Luther, ever one to speak his mind, said, 'It is a pity it ever got into the New Testament.'

> Revelation presents a wonderful picture of the Lord Jesus to encourage us, to cause us to worship and to help us face difficulties.

Although it contains seven wonderful letters to the churches, in chapters 1–3, it is usually classed not as a letter but as apocalyptic literature. The word 'apocalyptic' means 'an unveiling'. It is like seeing behind the stage while a play is going on. The book describes itself as a revelation. In other words, the curtain was drawn aside and John was able to see things normally concealed. He wrote them down for our benefit. He warns us, at our peril, not to alter it but to read it aloud.

Revelation presents a wonderful picture of the Lord Jesus to encourage us, to cause us to worship and to help us face difficulties. There are a whole variety of approaches to this book. Some believe that everything it says refers to events in the first century AD. Others that it covers the whole of history and we are living part of its story (the exact chapter varies!). Some believe it gives a detailed timetable for a future period still to come. Clearly, it does have an immediate reference to John's day, but, in general, it is a word to the church of every age.

Views of Revelation

1) Praeterist – a programme for early church history
2) Historicist – a programme for the whole of history
3) Futurist – a programme for the end of history
4) Idealist – a programme for all ages and every age

Here are principles that are valid for all generations. Some are illustrated from first-century events, others from historical incidents. We miss out when we confine their relevance to one specific period.

The book is a revelation, from God, to the churches of Jesus Christ. It is given in symbols, not pictures, because it was too dangerous to put it into words. Words can be too limiting anyway to convey what you want to say. So what is written needs to be interpreted not visualized, otherwise the result could be grotesque. This is not an unfolding film following a chronological sequence, but a series of slides from different angles. Here we have six different but parallel accounts of the whole of church history from the first to the second coming of Christ. In each presentation we learn how the church is to live when facing opposition. The fresh visions of Christ encourage us through it all.

> Here we have six different but parallel accounts of the whole of church history from the first to the second coming of Christ.

We can also divide Revelation into two halves, with chapters 1–11 telling the outside story of the church, and 12–22 telling the inside story, showing the spiritual significance of what is happening.

Let me mention three outstanding pictures of Jesus.

1. Chapters 1–3: Son of Man among the lampstands
   – here is Christ residing, addressing the inner life
   – to a sinful church he says, 'I know... repent'

2. Chapters 4–5: The throne and the Lamb
    – here is Christ reigning, addressing the outer conflict
    – to a doubting church he says, 'I have conquered... believe'

3. Chapter 19: Christ riding on a white horse
    – here is Christ returning, addressing ultimate destiny
    – to a fearful church he says, 'I am coming soon... endure'

The first speaks of Christ with us, here on earth among his churches. He knows what we face, understands our situation, and provides an honest and searching appraisal. There are words of encouragement and rebuke, of warning and hope. We are not alone. He is the head of the church

The second picture transports us to heaven. Here we see God's throne in a setting of worship. But the scroll of human destiny is held by the Lamb. Only he is qualified to break open the seals and rule over the affairs of peoples and nations.

The final picture is of Jesus riding on a white horse, coming back for his own with a crown on his head and a sword in his mouth. Against all the forces allied against the church, Christ will return. The future is secure.

So we have come to the end of the last book in our journey. The start of our journey back in Genesis seems a long time ago and the biblical story covers many generations. But at the end we have not lost sight of the beginning.

The Old and New Testaments both show the impact of one person, representing those who follow. In Adam, sin entered; in Christ, salvation came. Both were tempted, but, whereas Adam fell, Christ triumphed, even though he faced temptation in a wilderness while Adam was in paradise.

Both tell the story of a called-out people, the children of Israel and the church. They each had standards to live by, the Ten Commandments and the Sermon on the Mount. Both looked forward to a future, the Promised Land or our future inheritance in Christ. Both testaments ended with a great prophecy of a future coming.

Then there are a number of contrasts and comparisons between the opening chapters of Genesis and the final chapters of Revelation. Images recur – the Tree of life and the river. Instead of a man and a woman, husband and wife, we have Christ and his bride, the church, awaiting their marriage supper. The couple have become a community, as the garden becomes a city, the New Jerusalem. Paradise is not simply a place of innocence but one of holiness. Satan, triumphant in Eden, is now forever defeated. God once more dwells with his people. At last the tree of life, barred for so long, is available for its fruit to be tasted. Paradise lost has been restored. What a perfect end to a perfect book!

*   *   *

I hope that, after catching your breath, you will set off on your own hitch-hike through the Bible, visiting parts we had to hurry over, lingering over parts that interest you, and dipping into parts you have never looked at before. So thumbs out and begin your journey of a lifetime. Good travelling.